"This book serves as a practical and reflective tool to explore the importance of building connections and deepening knowledge of both our students and educational colleagues. Val and Kate explore the importance of building a sanctuary for our students through cultivating relationships. Their explicit focus on the power of language in creating community, engagement, and joy offers a refreshing perspective for educators to explore."

David Aderhold, *Superintendent of Schools and Educational Advocate*

"This book is a powerful reminder of the joy and passion for learning that both teachers and students will experience in a classroom based on trust, care, and vulnerability. Val and Kate's expertise and guidance will ignite (or reignite) the spark for educators to be braver, bolder, and more authentic with their students. The text is an incredible blend of linking theory to practice while engaging the reader as a reflective practitioner. A must read for pre-service and veteran educators alike!"

Dr. Jessica Monaghan, *Assistant Director of Teacher Preparation*

"As we enter this age of Artificial Intelligence, we must never forget that teaching is a profoundly human endeavor built upon the relationships between teachers and students. Kate and Val share years of valuable wisdom that will help both beginning and seasoned teachers unpack the complexities of building and supporting relationships that foster true growth and learning. There are many 'how to' books for teachers, but this is absolutely essential reading for any educator who wants to move from 'good' to 'great.' Their book provides the foundational building blocks for creating an authentic classroom culture that will empower teachers and students to reach their highest potential."

Todd Kent, *Teacher Educator*

"An inspiring, insightful guide to transforming life inside and outside the classroom that is at once a clearly written, practical manual. The authors draw on neurology, pedagogy, and experience, bridging theory and practice with personal anecdotes. The book makes a bold, convincing case that through authenticity and presence, we can engage our students as complete human beings, opening a space for real-time, life-altering learning and growth."

Emily Van Buskirk, *Rutgers University*

Transforming Teaching Through Relationship-Building and Self-Reflection

Creating connections with and among students is at the heart of all good teaching. In order to do this, we must identify and address the obstacles, conscious and unconscious, getting in the way of this goal. Authors Katherine M. Heavers and Valerie Kearns show how to build authentic relationships that focus on trust and voice while honoring the differences in individuals' experiences and learning styles.

This book covers topics such as fostering trust, wielding language with intention, nurturing emotional safety, offering meaningful feedback, unearthing and confronting bias, and promoting student voice. The authors encourage educators to do their own inner work to embrace vulnerability, which can help them to grow personally and, as a result, better nurture student growth. As a byproduct of this deep reflection, the authors intend for you to enjoy heightened psychological flexibility and experience more joy, both of which will enable you to better serve your students. Each chapter concludes with reflection questions and activities to support, challenge, and extend thinking.

Whether reading the book on your own or with colleagues, you will come away feeling supported on your journey as you strive to create meaningful connections that lead to lasting learning and empowered communities.

Katherine M. Heavers is currently a high school biology teacher and has served as an adjunct professor in teacher education at both Rutgers University and the College of New Jersey. She holds a Master's degree in science education and a Doctorate in social and philosophical foundations of education, both from Rutgers University.

Valerie Kearns has worked as a high school social studies teacher, professional development facilitator, and lecturer and clinical supervisor at Rutgers University Graduate School of Education. She holds a Master's degree in social studies education from Rutgers University.

Also Available from Routledge
Eye on Education
(www.routledge.com/k-12)

Passionate Learners, 3rd Edition: How to Engage and Empower Your Students
Pernille Ripp

Your First Year, 2nd Edition: How to Survive and Thrive as a New Teacher
Todd Whitaker, Katherine Whitaker, Madeline Whitaker Good

The Heart-Centered Teacher: Restoring Hope, Joy, and Possibility in Uncertain Times
Regie Routman

Classroom Management from the Ground Up
Todd Whitaker, Katherine Whitaker, Madeline Whitaker Good

The Student Motivation Handbook: 50 Ways to Boost an Intrinsic Desire to Learn
Larry Ferlazzo

Transforming Teaching Through Relationship-Building and Self-Reflection

Finding Our Way In

Katherine M. Heavers and Valerie Kearns

Taylor & Francis Group

NEW YORK AND LONDON

Designed cover image: Getty Images

First published 2025
by Routledge
605 Third Avenue, New York, NY 10158

and by Routledge
4 Park Square, Milton Park, Abingdon, Oxon, OX14 4RN

Routledge is an imprint of the Taylor & Francis Group, an informa business

© 2025 Katherine M. Heavers and Valerie Kearns

The right of Katherine M. Heavers and Valerie Kearns to be identified as authors of this work has been asserted in accordance with sections 77 and 78 of the Copyright, Designs and Patents Act 1988.

All rights reserved. No part of this book may be reprinted or reproduced or utilised in any form or by any electronic, mechanical, or other means, now known or hereafter invented, including photocopying and recording, or in any information storage or retrieval system, without permission in writing from the publishers.

Trademark notice: Product or corporate names may be trademarks or registered trademarks, and are used only for identification and explanation without intent to infringe.

ISBN: 978-1-032-80385-2 (hbk)
ISBN: 978-1-032-79810-3 (pbk)
ISBN: 978-1-003-49658-8 (ebk)

DOI: 10.4324/9781003496588

Typeset in Palatino
by KnowledgeWorks Global Ltd.

Dedications

For my two sons.
And for Jane.
KMH

For my babies,
who inspire me every day.
For Caylin, Eric, Iby, and Kaleef,
who are forever imprinted on my heart.
VK

Contents

Acknowledgments   xi

Introduction: The Keys to the Castle   1

PART I Strengthening Classroom Relationships   7

1. **Being Authentic:** How the Intentional Presentation of One's True Self Can Build Relationship in School Environments   9

2. **Considering the Power of Language as a Form of Connection:** How Communication Builds or Disrupts Classroom Relationships   18

3. **Building Trust:** How Intentional Vulnerability and Consistency Cultivate Connectedness   33

4. **Creating and Nurturing Emotional Safety:** How a Safe and Supportive Classroom Fosters Student Growth, Learning, and Empowerment   42

5. **Providing Meaningful Feedback:** How Intentional Communication Through Feedback Encourages Student and Educator Growth   63

PART II Looking Inward, Shining Out   85

6. **Increasing Our Self-Awareness:** How Self-Reflection and Present-Moment Awareness Transform Teaching and Learning   87

7. **Establishing Effective Working Relationships and Utilizing Accountability Partners:** How Collegial Relationships Improve Our Teaching   102

8. **Confronting Bias:** How to Identify, Reflect Upon, and Combat Types of Bias that Arise in Ourselves and in the Classroom   114

9 **Recognizing and Minimizing Stress:** How to Identify Stressors and Practice Stress-Management Techniques to Benefit Ourselves and Our Students   126

10 **Increasing Educator Flexibility:** How to Release Traditional Teacher Control to Strengthen Student-Teacher Connection   140

11 **Maximizing Student Voice and Choice:** How to Empower Students Through Greater Autonomy in the Classroom   154

12 **Learning Joy:** How to Be Intentional About Creating Opportunities of Joy for Ourselves and Our Students   165

   Conclusion: Sojourners Together   172

Acknowledgments

Writing this book has been a dream. We would both like to thank our editor, Lauren, who supported our work and made it all happen. We would also like to thank Hannah and Riya for their assistance in the details of book production. We are so grateful to those who provided endorsements and those who took the time to read the introduction and provide feedback, especially Bruce, Hugh, and Lisa.

Thank you to Jean and Bob for selecting us to chaperone the orchestra trip to Italy in 2014. Our bond, formed on that trip, led to the creation of this book.

We would like to thank the teachers who are *in it*. We see you. We respect you.

We would like to thank our colleagues, past and present. A special thank you goes to Amanda, our third HSM, for your friendship and support. You have helped each of us grow in the very best ways.

We also want to thank you, dear reader, for picking up this book. Thank you for the role you play in the lives of students and in the schools of this world. Remember that figuring out who you are takes time. We are excited to be on this journey with you.

And most importantly, thank you to each of our students. We are better people because of you.

KMH: It was the greatest gift to meet and befriend Valerie Kearns, as it is because of her exceptional expertise in the teaching of social studies, in addition to her determination and organizational skills, that the book in your hands became a reality.

My gratitude goes to Todd, Anne, and Jessica of Princeton's Teacher Preparation Program. They have made TPP home for me for nearly two decades and nurtured my teaching practice with unfailing support. They've also sent me some incredible student teachers, most especially Ariel, to whom my gratitude will always be most immense.

My gratitude to the formative teachers of my life – Gerry Hallgrimson, Peter Thompson, Penna Rose, and James Giarelli. I am the teacher I am today because of the unique impact each of you had upon me.

Miriam Robin, you taught me how to write lesson plans and be a public school science teacher. You taught me that every assessment should always *teach* something. Thank you for taking a chance on me.

My gratitude to the wonderful administrators, fellow teachers, and middle and high school counselors who all helped me learn to be a teacher. A huge thank you to my science colleagues and the teachers of Positivity Row who have always made me feel valued and loved. Special thanks to my friends Jen and Jenn. You are each incredible teachers. Keep going. Thank you for being you.

Holly and Haley, thank you for being my HAP sister-colleagues at our sister high school. We have created so much excellent work worth documenting and passing on to the next generation of teachers. Thank you for being my creative muses.

I thank the student who once told me to "take things with more grace," and every other brave student who, over the years, has had the courage to speak up and tell me how I could do better. My infinite gratitude to each and every one of you.

Thank you to Denise Bonnaig, my incredible yoga teacher of the last twenty years. *I am who I am and I love being me* because you told me, week after week, in your power yoga classes, "BE with you!" You taught me to be present in the pain and how to do hard things. You taught me how to *be*.

Thank you to my role model, Charlie, who is an incredible musician, music director, and talented teacher of math. I am so grateful you are my friend.

My gratitude to my Aunt Mary Ann. You are a splendid force, and I love you for your sheer willpower and brilliance. Thank you for all you have done for me and for my mom.

Thank you for always believing in me, Katie. Your steadfast love makes me strong.

My deep gratitude for my chosen family of childhood friends. Makara, you have never stopped loving me and supporting me. Hannah, you have seen me through a half century and I am eternally grateful for our lifetime of friendship. Thank you for your constant support and love.

My father, Richard, inspired me by spending his life as a teacher and showed me it was a highly effective way to influence the world for good. I give him thanks in the great beyond because he always supported my becoming a teacher.

Thank you to my brothers, Nathan and Ian. I have always been spurred on to improve, knowing you have long looked to me for courage. We have worked synergistically to get through this thing called life. I love you so much.

My gratitude to my mother, Barbara, who lived her life as a zoologist, teacher, and artist. An award-winning teacher, she was my inspiration in and out of the high school science classroom. I owe everything to Mama's vision: her passion, compassion, determination to live a good life, and her ever-present desire to make the world a better place.

Thank you to my two sons, Nathan and Éamonn. You have helped me to see the world in an entirely new light. You possess the power of the infinite within you! I love you each and I love you both.

I am most grateful to my beloved husband, Frank. You are a kind and brilliant person, the spouse I always dreamed of, and the one who sees me as I actually am. My deepest gratitude. I love you completely.

VK: I would like to express my gratitude to Kate for coming up with the idea to write a book together, emailing to say that "We just need to WRITE" on December 4, 2021. She has been an amazing source of support and encouragement for all my professional endeavors, and I am thankful for her presence in my life.

Thank you to John McNamara for hiring me for my first teaching job and for showing me what a genuinely supportive supervisor looks like. I will never forget your kind notes and your willingness to step in to lighten the burden of any teacher in your care.

Thank you to Beth Rubin, who has served as an inspiration for me throughout my graduate schooling and career. I have always appreciated your work and your guidance. I am so thankful that you offered me the opportunity to work with pre-service teachers, a position that filled my bucket when I needed it most.

Thank you to my colleagues-turned-friends, who gifted me with an amazing support system. You are truly "something awesome." Thank you, Nadra, for being the best mentor and source of support for *all* the issues that come with teaching and life. Thank you, Erin, for all the workshopping and conversations. You are brilliant and I feel like we have a few projects in the making. Thank you, AVID team of the 2020–2021 year, especially Sam and Michelle, for the support – we truly developed an "in it together" bond.

Thank you to everyone in the guidance department at my former teaching position for providing me with invaluable assistance in establishing and maintaining relationships with my students over the years. I know you all probably wanted to close your office doors when you saw me coming but (usually) didn't, and I am grateful.

I would also like to acknowledge and thank the wonderful teachers of my children who have made them feel loved and safe. Big shoutouts to Ms. Madhu, Ms. Rita, Ms. Tina, Ms. Mary, Ms. Allison, Ms. Taj, Ms. Jeeya, Ms. Pam, Ms. Martínez, Ms. Millie, Ms. Henríquez, Mrs. Murphy, and all those to come.

Thank you to my sister-friends, from high school and my 82 crew, for your encouragement and support in all the endeavors of my life.

I want to acknowledge two extraordinary women in my life: my Nanny and my Aunt Mary. These women, through their lifelong demonstrations of selfless kindness, shaped my understanding of how we can live in community with others. They showed me how to live with other people in mind. I feel lucky to have known them.

Thank you to my brother, Mikey, for being my earliest model of genius. Our brains work in very different and complementary ways, so I did your homework and you fixed my cars. I've always been able to see the genius in others because I first saw it in you, outside of the realm of school. Thank you also for giving me a supportive sister-in-law whom I cherish. Hopefully, she will read this aloud to you since I know you won't be reading it on your own.

Thank you to my dad, Mike, for always encouraging me to be a "squeaky wheel" and to agitate the things that need to be agitated. You have always fought for what is right, and I try to do the same.

Thank you to my mama, Jo Ann, for being my model of unconditional love and for teaching me to honor the humanity in every person. I appreciate you for all the big things and for all the things that might seem small. Your actions mean so much more than you know.

Finally, to my partner in life, Matt, I appreciate all you do. Thank you for providing me with the support and freedom to create and fulfill my life goals. And – my inspirations for it all – Alessia and Camillo, I love you. You have made my life more beautiful than I could have ever imagined.

Introduction

The Keys to the Castle

Every teacher has memorable moments unique to the profession. The student who cried in their arms after learning of a loss. The day their students surprised them with a baby shower. The student who slowly leaned back their chair to release a stream of spit on the floor. The student who shared that, instead of engaging in the lesson, he had counted each pimple on the teacher's face. The fear they felt on the day they realized that the announcement was not a drill. Every day holds surprises, and our handling of each unique moment of the job demonstrates our commitment to our students.

The profession of teaching is one of service, of community, and of love. Our health, physical and mental, is impacted by the levels of love and degrees of nurture we experience from the time we are born. As educators, we need to view our profession as a labor of love and recognize the very powerful impacts we can have on the lives of our students.

In a classroom, love looks like engagement, joyful laughter, curiosity, and question-asking. Love looks like bright eyes of wonderment, uninhibited silliness, and safety in structure. The goal is to nurture freedom of choice, freedom of being, and freedom of expression for both the learners and the teacher. This is the opportunity for everyone to be themselves and discover something new that helps them see and understand their place in the world. This is the chance to recognize that this place is unique, and they will not be judged for who they are in it. In a loving atmosphere, an educator fosters individual feelings of dignity and worth and therefore allows for the potential for lasting transformation. These positive experiences allow the students to integrate into a more whole version of themselves. They have felt what it feels like to be loved unconditionally, without any expectation of returned love, because that's not the purpose of the teacher's love. The teacher's love is offered freely – and forgiveness and understanding, too – because that is what growing human brains need.

The loving presence of a teacher can provide a sanctuary in which a learner exists in a place of already-enough-and-yet-becoming-the-next-version-of-themselves. As Maxine Greene eloquently expresses, "I am who I am not yet" (Pinar, 1998, p. 1). And so, "teaching [to intervene] in another's becoming," as Laverty (2006) says, is truly the greatest expression of love (p. 35). If you believe that what you can do will truly aid another in becoming all they are capable of growing into being, then you take your energy, time, and love and you pour it into the becoming of another. This is one of the most meaningful gifts a teacher can offer.

The topics we will discuss in this book aim to help educators create this supportive sanctuary for students. To establish this, we need to demonstrate authenticity and work to present ourselves in ways that build student trust. We need to use language, in our classroom communication and forms of feedback, that is accessible, values students' experiences, and honors students' strengths. We need to reflect on our own beliefs and behaviors and how they impact our relationships. These tasks may not be easy, but they are fundamental to the creation of a loving community that can allow for meaningful learning to occur.

As educators ourselves, we understand deeply the energy that it takes to do this profession well. A truly *good* educator does face the risk of burning out. Pouring so much love into others, and sustaining it year after year, is exhausting. And, of course, caring for each individual in our classrooms is only *one* of the seemingly endless tasks that must be completed each day. There are the administrative tasks – the lesson plans, faculty meetings, learning new technology systems – and the everyday necessities – the creation of lesson materials, responding to emails, and communicating with colleagues and families. These tasks take away time and energy, thus inhibiting us from investing more deeply in our students' lives. It often seems that there is an expectation for educators to be *everything* and know *everything*. This burden has become even more pronounced with the ever-evolving technologies with which we are expected to be familiar.

Stating our understanding of the realities of teaching is important because much of this book represents our ideal. We know that these ideal classrooms are out there, but we also know that the educators responsible for them are overworked and would never have the time to write a book, like this, that details their strategies. It is worth noting that Val's leaving full-time teaching was one of the main reasons we were able to do this ourselves. We fully understand the need for systemic changes, both at district levels and larger governmental levels, to allow for the type of classrooms we envision to be the norm rather than the exception. However, this is not to say that we cannot become better educators by engaging in the reflective exercises that we discuss in this book. While we might not always have the ability to change systems, we can start by working within the systems to best serve our students. And, just maybe, our new insights can push on these systems in ways that bring meaningful change.

As a way to recenter and reconsider our goals in the face of the realities of the profession, we believe that it is important to periodically remind ourselves of why we do the work we do. Why did we enter this profession? What did we hope we would achieve? Have these hopes changed and why?

Kate started teaching simply because she needed a job. Her father suggested she look into teaching before committing to the medical school path, leading to her first teaching job. There she experienced the first magical moment of joy that only comes after experiencing a class full of students perfectly in tune, learning, and being. Sitting in the classroom after that December school day had ended, feeling the echo of the buzzing life that had filled the room moments before, she realized there was no place she ever wanted to be than in a classroom. Moments like these – the joy felt when a class has just had a good shared laugh or engaged in a rich and transformative group discussion – have kept her passionate about teaching over the years. She cherishes the opportunities to cultivate meaningful student-teacher relationships (STRs) and student-student relationships (SSRs) and experience the never-ending growth that we are fortunate to enjoy in this profession.

When Val was five years old she declared, in her kindergarten exit interview, that she wanted to be a teacher. Throughout her years of schooling, her plan never changed. She has always recognized the responsibility of teachers, specifically social studies teachers, to help students develop effective citizenship skills. These skills – including those of expanding student understanding of perspective and developing empathy and the ability to connect with other humans – can help young people understand why atrocities and inequities persist and empower them to recognize and resist oppressive forces. She also recognized at a young age that, regardless of content, a teacher's presence and relationship with a student can have an immensely positive or negative impact on their life and life trajectory. In high school, she witnessed many of these examples, whether it was a teacher's suggestion of a career path that a student ultimately chose to follow or a teacher physically pushing a student out of the classroom for being late too many times, leading to his dropping out of school. She began to recognize that teachers who had a positive impact on students exhibited characteristics such as patience, kindness, empathy, authenticity, and enthusiasm, and she became further motivated to become one of those teachers who helped shape young people's lives for the better.

Val and Kate met while teaching at the same high school, but our first true bonding moments occurred while chaperoning an orchestra trip in Italy. One morning of the trip, we were so busy preparing the student orchestra for their show that we hadn't realized the time. We hadn't eaten yet and, by the time the students were ready, it was *riposo* and no eatery was open. A few hours later, we decided to sneak out to get something to eat, only to find that we were locked out of the venue. We sat there, pounding on what looked to us like castle doors, laughing in a situation where many would be angry and frustrated. That genuine show of our personalities in a time of potentially hangry discomfort (on our American Thanksgiving day in Europe) sealed the beginning of our friendship.

Little did we realize this image of a castle and the state of being shut out would take on such significant meaning for us in future years. The castle metaphor is one that involves the separation of some from others. That big, heavy wooden door was locked from the inside and we were the weary travelers seeking food and shelter. If we extend this metaphor to the institution of education, then we see education as a tool being used to wield power and to lock certain folks out of the castle. Our work seeks to rectify the inequality in connectedness between students and teachers. Teachers are the nearest interface; we are the ones making the day-in and day-out decisions about who gets our time, our focus, our attention, and our energy.

The system of higher education in this country also keeps folks out because only some teachers have the opportunity to become educated beyond their field. And even those who do obtain higher degrees are generally not able to keep themselves up-to-date on the latest innovations in technology for teaching, let alone the latest social and pedagogical theories, due to time and cost. What does this mean? Our focus on theory into practice is going to be a crucial piece of our book. We are able to do this only because we are each voracious readers. But even we, with our limited time and access, have to make choices and don't get to read nearly as much as we wish we could. We hope that this book can serve to provide some of the proverbial keys to unlock one of these "doors" we face as educators.

In the pages that follow you will find a guide to skill-building that has been informed by our research and personal experiences. We use our own experiences as asides throughout the book indicated by our initials (KMH and VK) to provide greater context in our own voices.

This ultimately is a book about building connections and deepening knowledge of our educator-human being selves. Through this exploration, we hope to empower anyone in the field of education who seeks to recognize their own wisdom from self-discovery and apply it to their professional role in the educational field.

Each chapter focuses on one skill that we believe educators need to examine and cultivate, whether a pre-service teacher considering these ideas for the first time or a veteran teacher looking to be reinspired and validated in their efforts. The chapter placement intentionally builds throughout the book, allowing educators to consider the foundation needed in order for meaningful learning and growth to occur. Chapters 1–5 focus on the importance of building strong relationships in the classroom and how these relationships can be cultivated. Chapters 6–12 ask the reader to turn inward, learn more about themselves in relationship to others, and reflect upon the individual and societal impacts of their personal and professional decisions.

At the end of each chapter, you will find suggested reflective activities. Our hope is that you engage with these activities in an open and honest way, ideally sharing your responses with a trusted friend or colleague. We intentionally leave space for you to note anything that strikes you or respond to any question we have posed.

We hope that you can connect to, and find meaning in, our writing and our experiences. Thank you for holding this book in your hands. We hope you enjoy your journey.

References

Laverty, M. (2006). Philosophy of education: Overcoming the theory-practice divide. *Paideusis*, 15(1), 31–44.

Pinar, W. F. (Ed.) (1998). *The passionate mind of Maxine Greene*. London & Bristol, PA: Falmer Press.

PART I
Strengthening Classroom Relationships

1

Being Authentic

How the Intentional Presentation of One's True Self Can Build Relationship in School Environments

We start with authenticity because we believe that it is, in fact, the starting point of a relationship. Cranton and Carusetta (2004) describe authenticity as "being genuine, showing consistency between values and actions, relating to others in such a way as to encourage their authenticity, and living a critical[ly reflective] life" (p. 7). Our definition of authenticity would include the ability to be comfortable in one's uniqueness and also comfortable in allowing others to see that uniqueness. When a person demonstrates authenticity, they are perceived as "real" and "genuine," someone worthy of trust and respect. We believe that meaningful relationships cannot be formed with people who hide their true selves, whether this is inadvertent or purposeful. How can one expect to form such a relationship with a person if they cannot, or are unwilling to, act in ways that represent their true feelings and values? And how can one build trust and connection with a person when they sense or discover superficiality or disingenuity in the other?

Rodgers and Raider-Roth (2006) discuss the phenomenon in which educators, especially pre-tenured educators, delineate a difference in their perception of themselves as *teachers* and themselves as *people*. As they note, "This distance between personal and professional selves can cause a tentativeness, beyond the tentativeness that naturally exists for new teachers, that undermines both their trust in themselves and, thereby, their students' trust in them" (p. 272). We agree that this portrayal of an inauthentic "teacher self" is damaging for oneself and their student-teacher relationships. Instead, we need to be committed to presenting our integrated whole selves in our professional lives.

It would be difficult – maybe even impossible – to reach a place of emotional safety in a classroom if the teacher were deemed to be inauthentic. So, even for those of us who view ourselves as genuine, we believe it is important to determine the ways in which we display our true selves and consider if we are doing so in a way that translates as such to our students. How can we then be sure we are being and *consistently displaying* our most authentic selves?

Recognizing One's Degree of Authenticity

We know from personal experience, and theory supports this, that deep reflection can lead to an identity that is more in line with a person's core beliefs. This is what we believe, and Laverty (2006) has shown, will change one's level of intentionality:

> And just as serious and responsible philosophical reflection leads to, and is constitutive of, living more authentically, I suggest the same is true for teaching. Serious and responsible philosophical reflection – enhanced by theoretical understanding – enables educators to engage with their respective disciplines, and others who are similarly engaged, with greater authenticity.
>
> By this I mean that teaching doesn't simply implement a set of procedures but also enlists and reveals the individual, both in his or her particularity and entirety. This makes the individual – in differentiation from the procedures which he or she employs – vulnerable to change … Teaching, then, is inextricably and inevitably connected with *who one is*, so that to think about one's teaching is to think about one's self.
>
> (pp. 32–33)

Picture a person you know who lives "authentically." What characteristics describe this person? We have compiled the following potentially adoptable characteristics that demonstrate genuineness. An authentic person may be recognized when they:

- give full credit in using the work of someone else – they tell the truth about the source of an idea or practice

- don't live in fear of judgment and make their decisions based upon what they know to be right and not based upon how they might be perceived by others
- try to see themselves as others see them only to ensure that they are not causing harm
- know that they are not fundamentally different from other humans and know how much there is to learn from the lives and worlds of others
- are not afraid of making mistakes because they know they are on a path to growth
- ask others for help because they recognize their own limitations
- listen to and heed the advice of others and then express gratitude for the learning opportunities
- act in ways, in all contexts of their life, that demonstrate alignment with their personal values and beliefs

While these traits may generically apply to an "authentic" person, it may be worthwhile to consider the traits that make *you* an authentic person. For example, in addition to the list above, Kate has developed a philosophy for living and a belief system that guides her daily, one in which she considers each morning as she starts the day. Each person will exhibit different characteristics in their displays of their true selves as reflected in their unique qualities.

It is important to acknowledge that what we hope to see may not be what we will find. Thus, as we seek to identify the authentic qualities of another, they may not match our ideal vision of what we hope to see. However, if we are able to see such qualities and recognize them as genuine to an individual, respect and positive relationships can begin to grow. Each of us has heard students discuss their respect for a teacher, despite aspects of that teacher's behavior they dislike, because they are able to recognize the authenticity of the teacher's personality. For example, a teacher might have a blunt way of speaking to others, or frequently hum during class, or present information in a manner that is not a student's preference. Despite qualities that may be deemed annoying or downright unpleasant, students were able to bond with these teachers, as they found their presentation of their true selves to be most important.

We also recognize that demonstrating our true selves may reveal aspects that are not necessarily beneficial for building relationships. Our hope is that by engaging in the latter portion of this book in which we ask you to reflect by looking inward, you will be able to identify and address any areas that may pose difficulties in your professional relationships.

The Importance of Authenticity in the Classroom

Through our conversations with students over the years, we have become aware of the value students place on authenticity. We have also come to know how perceptive students can be in identifying when adults are hiding or masking something. They will quickly identify a teacher as "fake," know when a teacher has "favorite" and "least favorite" students or doesn't actually know the answer to their question, and they *always* know when a teacher is hiding a pregnancy.

Students want a teacher who will be honest and vulnerable. They want someone "real" whom they can trust. Connections are built when a teacher tells the students when they are having a bad day, admits that they do not know something, or they have made a mistake. A teacher does not need to overshare to accomplish this, but masking their truth, for whatever reason, will likely translate as a breach of trust for students.

We would argue that a demonstration of authenticity needs to occur early in the year. A student's understanding of a teacher's true self will grow over time, but we believe that teachers need to be intentional and vulnerable right away. Reflecting upon each of our own interaction styles served as an example of the importance of this. Kate's openness is immediately apparent upon meeting her, and Val is typically guarded, which may appear as someone who is hiding her true self. Because of Kate's comfortability in vulnerability, Val was disarmed and reciprocated that vulnerability in their first conversation. Recognizing that Val's guarded nature can be lifted with a genuine show of openness allowed each of us to consider how that knowledge could impact our relationships with others and our relationships in the classroom. This highlighted the importance of taking the first step to disarm those who are similarly guarded.

Communication data from our students has served as further support that those who were deemed to be honest, vulnerable, and authentic early in the year made the students feel more comfortable in their classrooms. Similarly, Johnson and LaBelle (2017) found that college students associate "authentic teaching" with instructors who are approachable, passionate, attentive, capable, and knowledgeable. They, like other researchers, conclude that "teachers should strive to demonstrate authenticity in their communication with students" (p. 435).

The Role of Self-Acceptance

It is important to acknowledge that being authentic – being your true self in all the areas of your life – may require some soul-searching and reflection. It requires the confidence and strength to be vulnerable even when it might be uncomfortable.

While we may not expect students to have a high level of confidence in vulnerability yet, we can expect this of adults, especially those who have chosen to be in the field of education. At the very least, we need adults in the field who recognize the importance of vulnerability and are committed to trying their best. But we do recognize that one needs self-acceptance to want to *be* oneself. Each of us knows individuals who have unresolved traumas that have prevented them from connecting with, and loving, their true selves. Consequently, this prevented them from fully connecting with others. Because the effectiveness of this profession centers on relationship, self-acceptance has a unique importance in the efficacy of an educator.

We believe that acceptance of self – essentially an ability to love and show yourself compassion – gives us the confidence to accept and utilize feedback and to give up control in the classroom. This allows for the space for self-improvement and the type of teaching that can inspire change. Knowing, and being comfortable with, our own identities is an important piece of being an authentic human. While we will discuss this in greater depth later in this book, we want to recognize the importance of being authentic with ourselves before we can be authentic with others. However, we may not feel safe to reveal every aspect of our identities in our professional lives. We know from our own teaching lives that some revelations take time. These could be life-changing events, illnesses, losses, or one's own sexual orientation or gender identity. We also know that there may be parts of our identities that we may never reveal.

So, while we recognize the importance of presenting our authentic selves in the classroom, we also recognize how societal privilege and emotional and physical safety play a role. We believe that educators need to be as authentic as they can safely and comfortably be in front of their students.

Creating Opportunities to Demonstrate Authenticity

In some cases, we may need to create opportunities to reveal our authentic selves. Val, for example, chooses to demonstrate vulnerability on the first day by sharing personal and medical information with students, explaining how they may impact her presence in the class. We have also allowed opportunities for students to ask us questions about our lives, whether in times of lesson transition or at the beginning or conclusion of a class. There are also times when intentionally including personal experiences can enhance the effectiveness of a lesson.

Kate (Heavers, 2012), in her doctoral dissertation, writes about how the "telling break," a type of educational interruption, provides an opportunity for educators to demonstrate authenticity:

> There are benefits to experiencing a teacher's stories, personal anecdotes and emotional revelations. Even the angry outburst occasionally wakes us up and brings us back to an awareness we might have lost. Existing in the space together becomes the real life of the classroom; everything else is the continuity, the background noise, the place where we lose ourselves 'in the white space between the little blue lines,' as [one student] says.
>
> (p. 179)

When we take the time to tell, we are allowing the students to see us as human. The teacher is also able to view the students as more human, because in the act of listening we are reminded of their whole humanity, too. The dynamic of the classroom shifts. The power differential is on pause. The space opens up for a moment where the roles drop away. It serves as a moment of relief for both the students and the teacher, and it brings a sense of togetherness. Here, the authentic nature of the teacher allows for a connection-building sense of peace and respite from the ever-present curricular requirements.

Cayanus, Martin, and Goodboy (2009) researched the impacts of instructor self-disclosure (one type of the telling break) on college-aged students. They found that when such self-disclosures were seen as relevant to the course content, "students seemingly are more motivated to play an active role in the learning process," and they "view relevant self-disclosures as their teachers' attempts to create a positive, open learning environment" (p. 111). These opportunities allow for benefits in both learning and relationship-building.

Another way to demonstrate authenticity is through maintaining consistency in one's behaviors and actions. Cranton and Carusetta (2004) acknowledge the importance of consistency in another's determination of an educator's authenticity, suggesting that educators "should practice what they preach and be sure not to espouse one way of working and then behave in a different way in their own teaching" (p. 7). In our teaching experiences, we have similarly found that such consistency in behavior serves as a way to demonstrate our true selves, as moments where we act in unexpected ways (without explanation) can be perceived as a false persona. For example, if we say that a certain behavior is permitted in class and then reprimand a student who engages in this behavior, this would be viewed as a case in which a teacher was inauthentic in their initial communication. And, as any of us who work with children know, one perceived instance of disingenuity can have long-term impacts.

Ultimately, as Johnson and LaBelle (2017) note, "The process of teaching authentically need not be more complicated than making simple and direct statements regarding the level of concern and care that a teacher holds for their students" (p. 436). Ensuring that students feel like their teacher sees them as individuals, and ensuring that the teacher presents themselves in a way that is integrated, rather than split between a professional and personal self, are key to one's presentation as authentic.

Authenticity will not just enhance our effectiveness as a teacher but is also a secret to happiness in many areas of our lives (Boyraz, Waits, & Felix, 2014; Brunell et al., 2010; Goldman & Kernis, 2002; Sheldon, Ryan, Rawsthorne, & Ilardi, 1997; Wang, 2016). There is harmony of being when who we want to be *theoretically* matches who we want to be *practically*. If there is a huge discrepancy between who we are and what we are doing, we are going to end up being physically and mentally depleted and maybe even become physically ill.

Being vulnerable enough to be truly authentic with students is not without risks, however. There is the potential to be hurt in any situation in which we invest our energies. We know that, specifically working with teenagers, emotional risk is always high. If you step into true connection with them, you also have to walk a very fine line from both a legal and emotional standpoint. This means that we need to have, and communicate, a clear understanding of our role in their lives and the boundaries that always must be upheld. However, this need to maintain safety cannot be a reason to avoid connection-building. Teaching is not an easy job but many (most? all?) of us enter the profession to positively impact the lives of children, and this is only possible if we are willing to invest ourselves fully.

In sum, an educator cannot only teach content, and similarly, it would be awkward and inappropriate to teach a lesson about ourselves. Instead, we need to find the crevices in the castle walls which let the light in. These are the moments and spaces where there are opportunities to reveal more of our authentic selves. We should strive to be more authentic – genuine, true – versions of ourselves to be role models for our students of kindness, compassion, passion for learning, and forgiveness.

Reflective Activities

- Identify someone in your life that you would consider authentic/real/genuine and consider how this person makes you feel. Then identify someone in your life that you do not consider to be genuine. Discuss differences in how you act around each person.

  _____
  _____
  _____

- Ask yourself the following questions:
  - Do you feel like you can be your authentic self in front of others? In front of students?

  _____
  _____
  _____

  - What factors prevent you from being fully authentic?

  _____
  _____
  _____

- Ask a trusted person in your life the following question: "How do you perceive me?"
  - Does their description match with your self-views?

  _____
  _____
  _____

References

Boyraz, G., Waits, J. B., & Felix, V. A. (2014). Authenticity, life satisfaction and distress: A longitudinal analysis. *Journal of Counseling Psychology, 61,* 498–505.

Brunell, A. B., Kernis, M. H., Goldman, B. M., Heppner, W., Davis, P., Cascio, E. V., & Webster, G. D. (2010). Dispositional authenticity and romantic relationship functioning. *Personality and Individual Differences, 48,* 900–905.

Cayanus, J., Martin, M., & Goodboy, A. (2009). The relation between teacher self-disclosure and student motives to communicate. *Communication Research Reports, 26,* 105–113.

Cranton, P., & Carusetta, E. (2004). Perspectives on authenticity in teaching. *Adult Education Quarterly, 55,* 5–22. https://doi.org/10.1177/0741713604268894.

Goldman, B. M., & Kernis, M. H. (2002). The role of authenticity in healthy psychological functioning and subjective well-being. *Annals of the American Psychotherapy Association, 5,* 18–20.

Heavers, K. (2012). *Toward a theory of the educational interruption: A conceptual model of the telling break.* https://doi.org/doi:10.7282/T3B27T7M

Johnson, Z. D., & LaBelle, S. (2017). *An examination of teacher authenticity in the college classroom.* Communication Education.

Laverty, M. (2006). Philosophy of education: Overcoming the theory-practice divide. *Paideusis, 15*(1), 31–44.

Rodgers, C. R., & Raider-Roth, M. B. (2006). Presence in teaching. *Teachers and Teaching: Theory and Practice, 12,* 265–287. https://doi.org/10.1080/13450600500467548

Sheldon, K. M., Ryan, R. M., Rawsthorne, L. J., & Ilardi, B. (1997). Trait self and true self: Cross-role variation in the big-five personality traits and its relations with psychological authenticity and subjective wellbeing. *Journal of Personality and Social Psychology, 73,* 1380–1393.

Wang, Y. N. (2016). Balanced authenticity predicts optimal well-being: Theoretical conceptualization and empirical development of the authenticity in relationships scale. *Personality and Individual Differences, 94,* 316–323.

2

Considering the Power of Language as a Form of Connection

How Communication Builds or Disrupts Classroom Relationships

As we write this book, we are reminded of the importance of writing in an accessible and relatable way. We wanted to remain grounded in our experiences and allow educators to identify themselves in at least some part of our writing. While we discuss theory, we are purposeful in maintaining focus on classroom practice rather than becoming too abstract – hopefully we have achieved this! We recognize ideal scenarios but also the reality of day-to-day classroom experiences and district and state level constraints, and we do our best to discuss teaching strategies that apply regardless of individual teaching circumstances.

We alternate between the use of "teacher" and "educator" throughout the book as these terms are most familiar to us, but we mean to refer to all those who educate in any capacity, not only those confined to the role of teacher. We also try our best to use language that is inclusive and affirming. If we have not, we welcome the feedback, as we aim to adjust our language continuously to match that which reflects the preferred terms of all people.

We wanted to address language early in the book as our communication with students will be one of the first ways in which we show ourselves to them. Our language displays our comfort levels, our biases, our understanding, our caring, and our support. The words we use communicate so much more than what we necessarily mean to say. Because of this, it is important to reflect upon our language choices and build our own language skills if we want to create a foundation to build strong relationships.

Accessibility of Language in the Classroom

Let's address comprehension first. Our students need to *understand* what we are saying. As basic as it might sound, the very first thing we must consider is whether the pace of our speech and the words coming out of our mouths allow students to understand what we are attempting to communicate. Our communication needs to be in language they can understand.

Each of us has had the experience of teaching multilingual learners and, over time, understood the importance of reading student body language to determine, in part, their level of comprehension. While this phenomenon is certainly not limited to students learning English, the opportunity to teach these multilingual students helped each of us to be highly reflective. It forced us to be more aware of the ways in which we needed to improve our communication in the classroom. We have noticed that a student leaning back in their chair with their eyes scanning the faces of their peers is a common indicator the teacher may have lost their attention. Other indicators may be a rise in noise level, general agitation of the group, or a sudden surge in the number of students asking to go to the bathroom. At a time like this, the first thing to do is to ask oneself "When and where did I lose them?" While it may seem obvious at times, we cannot overlook the importance of using accessible language in the classroom. In the absence of a brave student who shouts "You are losing us!" we need to be mindful of the nonverbal cues.

Strategies that have greatly benefited our teaching have included the following:

- defining terms for everyone in writing
- pausing while speaking to allow students to write notes
- using visuals and/or graphic organizers to accompany concept explanations
- normalizing technology use for defining and explaining vocabulary
- pausing the lesson or video to check for understanding (and ensuring full class participation in these checks)
- consistently using closed captioning on videos
- making translating tools readily available
- asking for students to repeat instructions or summarize concepts learned

We note the need for district support and recognition of the talents of multilingual students. Each district should have experts available, as we did/do in our district, to assist general education teachers in making their lessons and assessments more accessible.

Using Identity-Affirming Language

Once we have addressed comprehension, there are other barriers to consider in terms of the language we use to interact with our students. Over the years, many students have shared with us that one of the biggest disruptors in a relationship with a teacher was their unfamiliarity with the student's identity group, as evidenced through their use of language. While it is understandable to be unfamiliar with identity groups that are different from our own, especially if we do not have personal experience with individuals from those backgrounds, there is much a teacher can do to remedy this. First, a teacher can always make an effort to learn more about each and every student in the class. This can help prevent an individual student or a small group of students from feeling responsible for being the sole representatives of their identity group.

Safe, supportive relationships will be difficult to build with students if we are not referring to their identity groups in the ways that they do. Showing unfamiliarity with language related to a student's identities can be othering, especially when it is a continued practice where the teacher demonstrates no effort to learn. Conversely, when a teacher uses language that *matches* the students' identities, this indicates familiarity with a given group and/or effort and serves as validation. This applies to everything from the names of groups of people to the appropriate use of personal pronouns. This will require some learning, as language and culture are ever-changing, and will likely require practice. While familiarizing ourselves with identity group language may be time-consuming and initially uncomfortable, it is an important step in building relationships. A good starting place for knowledge of appropriate language as it relates to identity groups is the Bias-Free Language section in APA Style and Grammar Guidelines, found at https://apastyle.apa.org/style-grammar-guidelines/bias-free-language. We can model learning as teachers for our students in a way that will nurture a more accepting classroom environment and make us relatable at the same time. This will, in turn, allow our students to grasp the importance and necessity of appropriate language use, not just for the issues in our particular classroom, but at a societal level.

Even before addressing identity groups, a potential relationship-building or relationship-disrupting moment occurs when we first voice a student's name. Our willingness to use the student's preferred name and pronunciation speaks volumes. As we are sure most educators can relate, since we certainly can, name pronunciation can be difficult in the case of unfamiliar names. We, too, are very much acquainted with the feelings of shame and inadequacy in our inability to pronounce certain sounds in our students' names. As Bucholtz discusses in her essay "On Being Called Out of One's Name: Indexical Bleaching as a Technique of Deracialization" (in Alim, Rickford, &

Ball, 2016), misnaming a student can have impacts that are traumatizing and dehumanizing. Bucholtz suggests some strategies to help in the classroom:

1. Don't remark on the unusualness of a name or its spelling. Don't ask about the origin …. Avoid treating some names as normative and others as non-normative.
2. Ask people how they prefer you address them, and always address them that way …. Never use a nickname or otherwise adapt or change someone's name without their explicit indication that this new name is welcome.
3. Make the effort to correct your ignorance; don't expect the bearer of the name to do the work for you ….
4. Finally, if you remain in doubt … simply ask – politely and apologetically. Never blame someone for their name (pp. 286–287).

To expand on points three and four above, excessive apologizing can cause discomfort for the student. We should not put a student in the position of trying to make us feel better about our inability to pronounce their name, publicly or privately. As in all relationships, the effort matters. If we are explicit with the student about our intention to pronounce their name to the best of our ability then the student will notice. If we continue to fail, we cannot give up. If we are able to sit in our discomfort, this will have positive dividends in our relationship with the student. Since an entire class may be watching, it benefits us to remember that we are sending a positive message to every onlooker; each of them matters too, and we will help to show them our dedication to meeting each of their needs.

In our classrooms, asking students to state their names for introduction and attendance purposes has allowed us and the rest of the class to hear each student's preferred name and pronunciation. We make notes on the pronunciation if we are accustomed to pronouncing the name differently or if it is a name with which we are unfamiliar. We each have had students, months or years later, gently remind us that our pronunciations were off. After the initial feelings of shame, we felt grateful that they allowed us the opportunity to correct ourselves, and then we practiced.

Beyond names, the way in which we talk about groups of people can be either affirming or alarming to students and colleagues. For example, although there have been efforts to reconsider deficit language in the field of education, many of us would likely still find words like "low-functioning," "non-English speaker," and "at risk" to be commonly used in school settings. Rather than using functioning labels (e.g. "low-functioning"), we can refer to the level of support needed ("a person with high support needs"). We can refer to language in terms of assets ("multilingual student/learner") and we can use language that recognizes structural issues that face students as opposed to suggesting that the problem lies with the person themselves ("historically underserved" vs. "at risk"). Regarding ability levels, person-first language is generally a good rule, although many individuals and communities prefer identity-first language, notably the deaf, blind, and autistic communities (American Psychological Association, 2022; Centers for Disease Control and Prevention, 2022).

The use of positive language in the classroom can further extend to how we refer to our students overall ("learners" or "scholars"), our classroom activities, or our assessments. The AP program Val taught for years referred to assessments as "opportunities." While introducing the term may have resulted in some initial eye-rolling, Val found it helpful to be able to use such positive, growth-oriented language in an otherwise stress-inducing course.

Addressing Content Language

The importance of language also extends to content topics, as it can indicate a deep understanding, or alternately a whitewashed cis-heteronormative misunderstanding, of the experiences of historically (and systemically) marginalized groups.

KMH: While language is a social construct, the factual nature of science doesn't always leave room for the full experience of being human. In the following examples, we can learn how important it is to recognize the powerful impacts of our own biases and biases previously embedded in curricula.

In one example, I once talked in class about a "mother," and a student corrected me saying, "I think it would be better to say 'a person with a uterus'." I was grateful for that correction and have been more careful using the language surrounding parenthood ever since.

As another example, when a teacher is describing the effects of physical exertion on the human body, they might unconsciously describe an increase in heat or the vasodilation of capillaries in the face as blushing. However, this would indicate the teacher's automatic assumption that the human they are talking about is white. People with darker skin, however, might display the effects of physical exertion through sweat alone and experience a slight darkening of the face. In a similar way, a person with dark skin will indicate the absence of oxygen with a grayish or whitish shift in hue around the mouth while, for a white person, the face instead will turn blueish.

VK: When referring to historical content, we need to use terms that accurately portray the experiences of the impacted group. Some examples include the use of "incarceration camp" vs. "internment camp" when discussing the experience of Japanese Americans in the 1940s and "massacre" vs. "battle" when discussing the encounters between the U.S. Army and the Lakota people at Wounded Knee. This means we need to acknowledge textbook bias. Lessons in which we explored textbook bias have been some of the most meaningful and engaging lessons for my students. Many of the American history textbooks I have been assigned for my courses over the years have included inappropriate references to a number of different groups of people. Most obviously, when the authors write "Americans" they are referring generally to white Christian cisgender heterosexual middle-income Americans, effectively making this group the default group and anyone outside of this group an "other."

As educators, we need to acknowledge how groups of people experience events differently and help students analyze the reasons why. We also need to ensure that we are consistently using humanizing language when discussing humans and correct student vocabulary when necessary, for example, "enslaved" as opposed to "slave" or "undocumented" as opposed to "illegal."

Choosing to Adapt One's Language

We each are fascinated with the way that language evolves and how words and phrases can be used to communicate so much more than just the words we are saying. Phrases we use, whether or not we are aware, can identify our political affiliations, our likes and dislikes, and our comfort/familiarity levels with a topic or group. We each feel compelled to research any word or phrase that sounds potentially offensive (e.g. "no can do," "master bedroom") to see if we should change our language, and then we do!

Unfortunately there is a (not so new) trend occurring which Val refers to as *privileged language apathy* in which some Americans (generally, but not always, white, cisgender, straight, able-bodied Americans) refuse to adjust their language to the accepted terms for historically marginalized communities. These people perceive it a "burden" to adjust their language and would rather use terms, or pronunciations, that make them feel comfortable at the expense of others. Their language effectively excludes and suggests their apathy about the impacts of their decisions upon others. This disregard for other humans has no place in education. We work with students during their formative years. Such dehumanizing actions can traumatize and negatively impact children in ways that can have lasting and lifelong effects.

VK: I have had the experience of working with individuals (both adults and students) who seemingly harbored this *privileged language apathy*. Most of these individuals had very little contact with those outside of their identity groups and therefore felt that the impact on others was exaggerated. For a number of these individuals, hearing the perspectives of people hurt by language that they used served as a "lightbulb moment." I do not know definitively whether these moments were enough to inspire them to change their language for the long term. I *do* know that providing a space for people to share their experiences was beneficial both to those who do not spend time in diverse settings as well as those who rarely feel comfortable talking about their identities. Those folks with limited experience had their horizons widened while those who had the experience of being othered felt validated. A number of these individuals expressed gratitude for the opportunity to learn and/or be heard and guilt for having lived so many years without this knowledge.

I have also had experiences with individuals who defended, and even seemed to proudly proclaim, their *privileged language apathy*. For these individuals there was a clear desire to defend themselves and their ways of operating. They wanted others to adjust to their way of speaking, claiming that these people needed to be "tougher," "less sensitive," or "less emotional." They chose to disregard that changing something about oneself is an admirable and often tough task.

As we will discuss later in the book, neuroplasticity allows for changes to be made to any of our behaviors, language included. People *can* change their language, but they need to *want* to do so. As educators, this decision should be easy, and, as with most skills in this book, modeling our language choices to students serves as a powerful opportunity for learning.

The Importance of Nonverbal Language

It is also important to recognize and communicate to students that language extends to the ways in which we communicate that go beyond words themselves and involve the full expression of brain-into-muscle. Our neural traces ensure that our emotions will be communicated whether or not we use our words to communicate them. Our bodies – the tightening of the jaw, the pace of our speech, our volume, the intonation in our words – will release what we are actually thinking, unless we take the care to intentionally shape our expressions and consider the receivers of them.

Val often finds herself speaking with her daughter about tone. She reminds her that the way in which we say things can be more important than what we say. She will frequently ask, "Is that the right tone to use?" Val asked this of her daughter so frequently that she found her daughter began to question tone herself. Recently she noted, "Well you don't *seem* happy about it." She was right – Val wasn't really happy.

Our emotions show our degree of awareness through our voice and tone. It is important to keep this truth front and center in all our relationships, including those with students. We need those listening to us to trust what we are telling them. When we admit our honest emotions, we are helping our students to integrate a tone change they may experience in our voice. This builds trust. Think of your lexicon of language as comprised of words. Think of a lexicon of *tone*. No one has yet created a dictionary of tones, but the students are quickly able to note incongruencies in our words and our emotions. For example, while we appreciate sarcasm, we have seen it go wrong frequently enough that we believe it should be used sparingly in a classroom, if at all. If we do choose to use sarcasm with a group, we can acknowledge this aloud, since each individual reads sarcasm differently, and some do not recognize it at all.

Some teachers use a voice and tone altogether different from their authentic ones when teaching, essentially a "teacher voice." As we have argued thus far, we need to remove our "masks" as much as possible when facing students. Acting like a "teacher" and using a contrived voice, rather than just being ourselves, will make us less effective, as we will not read as genuine. As a result, our students may find us unworthy of earning their trust (Rodgers & Raider-Roth, 2006). While the students may never explicitly tell us this, they will maintain their distance to protect themselves.

Supporting Student Language Skills

As educators, helping students to learn appropriate language skills as they relate to identity groups is important in so many ways. It can be validating for individual students, it can help students to build relationships with others, and it can also help to prevent our students from becoming adults who are apathetic to the needs of others.

We also need to help our students use language to communicate their needs to us and to their classmates. Sentence starters can, and should be, used to build academic language in writing and discussions but also can be very effective in helping students to express feelings effectively in social situations. Providing students with statement options can also be helpful. For example, teaching students that saying "What you said makes me feel uncomfortable," "That doesn't sit right with me," or a simple "Ouch!" can indicate their discomfort and allow them time and space to figure out whether and how they might want to address the situation.

Teachers have great power in modeling these communication lessons to their students. Val has always appreciated Kate's intentionality with language, both inside and outside of the classroom.

KMH: We humans use language intentionally to wield power. Since we are not born with language in our brains, because it is learned through the degree of nurture and instruction we receive, it can be an acquisition flex to wield it with the greatest skill. This is because it is a flex of the acquisition of education, of privilege, of opportunity, of networks of enrichment to which one is exposed. We equate the capacity to speak well with the capacity to think well. It is a way to stand out and a tool to navigate the world. Language matters when you are trying to save someone's life, when you are trying to save a friendship, and when you are communicating emotion. I have always recognized this power in language, and I try to convey its importance to my students.

Language allows you to choose your level of clarity and how you want to be perceived. I never used to tell my students "we have about ten minutes left" when I knew that we had twelve. I was compulsively precise because it was more true, and I have always used language as a way to convey the truth. I have learned that meticulous precision is not what is necessary. Rather, being less precise can be a softer and gentler way of being and can set folks at ease. I am learning that our use of language allows us to be both true *and* kind. It is a life quest of mine to be more tactful, which I explain to my students as "telling the truth with kindness."

As another example, in response to a student's use of the phrase "my fault," Kate has begun to suggest the phrase "my brain, my process" instead. She explains that the phrase "my brain, my process" removes the shame associated with not meeting an expectation of another and indicates an acceptance of different paths of learning. This reframing of a common saying is a perfect example of Kate's intentionality in language and one that can be modeled in the classroom.

Kate also brings this intentionality to teaching the language surrounding boundaries. She encourages students to set boundaries in their relationships as a way to communicate their needs, including in their student-teacher relationships. For example, one of her students recently indicated that she didn't want Kate to read the personal letter she had written to her sister during an assignment in which students wrote a letter of advice surrounding lifestyle and nutritional choices. Here, the student deemed her advice too personal for her teacher's eyes. She indicated to Kate that it would betray her sister's trust if she revealed details of her life to her classroom teacher. Rather than demanding to read the letter to determine whether the assignment had been properly completed, Kate respected and praised this request, and the student instead gave the rubric to a friend to get feedback. Kate teaches students to use language to identify and maintain safe and healthy boundaries in the classroom, thus validating the importance of this academic and life skill.

How to Value Student Expression While Considering Grading and Curricular Constraints

Despite our best efforts to value and praise students' use of language, we may unintentionally devalue it. As teachers, we need to adhere to curricular and state standards and likely are expected to teach and/or grade grammar. We may also be limited in language resources for multilingual students. But do these constraints allow room for a student's full talents, expression, and creativity? What is the best way to strike the balance between structure, bureaucratic standards, and a student's spoken and written capabilities and creativity?

VK: In hooks' essay "Language: Teaching New Worlds/New Words" (1994), she discusses one soul-grabbing line from Adrienne Rich's poem "The Burning of Paper Instead of Children." The line reads, "This is the oppressor's language yet I need it to talk to you" (p. 167; full poem available at https://poetrysociety.org/poems/the-burning-of-paper-instead-of-children). While my first introduction to this poem was in hooks' *Teaching to Transgress*, I was also moved by the quote, enough to locate and read Rich's beautiful poem.

The quote reminded me of my experiences teaching AP US History and, specifically, the writing rubric set by the College Board at the time I taught the course. The essays were graded based on a

0–9, and the criteria for the highest scores (8–9) required an essay to be "well organized and well written" but "may contain minor errors that do not detract from the quality of the essay." The 5–7 essay "has acceptable organization and writing" and "may contain errors that do not seriously detract from the quality of the essay," and the 2–4 essay "may be poorly organized, poorly written, or both" and "may have major errors" (College Board, 2014). I had always wondered what *really* made the essays "well organized" and "well written" and whether some of my strongest writers, those with unique writing flair, might score poorly if someone did not value their writing style. As a result of these nebulous criteria, I found myself playing it safe by encouraging students to limit their creativity. I thought it was in their best interest to restrain their writing to fit a more standardized style, simply to please the graders.

I was reminded how conflicted I felt about this rubric when, just yesterday, I had a conversation with a former colleague about how to help a student prepare for the writing portion of the AP test. In my teaching, I generally preferred students to write their responses using the language in which they felt the most comfortable. However, when teaching AP courses for which an exam had strict writing expectations and when preparing for district assessments that placed a higher (and in some cases great) importance on students' use of "standard English" grammar, I enforced those standards.

This style of writing, which really is just that – a style that those in power agreed would represent the culture of this country during any particular time period – could be considered the "oppressor's language" by some in our rooms, or perhaps by all if we analyzed it enough. It has been given power by educators (and businesses) in this country as we continue to teach it as the preferred and "proper" mode of speech.

I recognize that one of the purposes of school is to prepare students for the "real world" and that this adherence to the conventions of "standard English" grammar reflects what students would likely find in the business world in this country. (I am currently writing in conventional "standard English!") At the same time, I never wanted to devalue the ways in which my students naturally spoke and wrote so I, like many other teachers, emphasized the importance of writing for different audiences. I would provide feedback on grammar only on assessments written for outside audiences, in cases where I was providing English language instruction, or when the writing was unclear. Even in those cases, I had conflicting feelings.

With my students, I have found it valuable to have discussions about exploring the oppressive structures that led to the valuing of different forms of language above others. This has helped me explain my classroom choices but, more importantly, it helped my students to think about the power of language. As Alim notes in the epilogue titled "Sorry to Bother You: Deepening the Political Project of Raciolinguistics," the goal of educators should not be to "stick to the script" to achieve success (Alim, Rickford, & Ball, 2016). Instead, we should teach students the "script" as a tool and encourage them to question its value for themselves, which can effectively serve as one means by which students can confront oppressive forces they encounter.

As a result of the educational laws in certain states, some educators are not able to explicitly recognize the full value of the dialects and languages of those who sit in our classrooms. Despite this, we need to indicate the value of the many dialects and languages of our students in ways that are genuinely validating. Not only should we, as educators, reflect upon this, we should discuss it openly with students. hooks (1994) recognizes that by changing "conventional ways of thinking about language" and "creating spaces where diverse voices can speak in words other than English or in broken, vernacular speech," we purposefully allow for useful moments of unfamiliarity and inaccessibility for some individuals (pp. 173–174). We would argue that these are the moments where we build relationships and community, the moments of comfort and authenticity on the part of the speaker, and the moments in which temporary discomfort on the part of the unfamiliar audience leads to learning and growth. These learning opportunities should be supported by district policy and district funding in the form of dual language classes, translating services, and resources that reflect linguistic and cultural diversity. Our encouragement of our students' natural forms of communication in the classroom is one way in which we can teach in a "culturally sustaining" manner, one in which educators "meaningfully value and maintain the practices of their students in the process of extending their students' repertoires of practice to include dominant language, literacies, and other cultural practices" (Paris, 2012, p. 95).

We need to move beyond deficit approaches and view students' cultural assets for what they are if we want students to feel affirmed. Our explicit communication of the value of one's expression is powerful in the classroom. It is our responsibility to acknowledge and respect each individual's life experience and learning that have shaped who they are as they enter our classroom. In doing so, we make them most open to more learning.

Our communication with students is arguably the single most important way that we teach them to become successful communicators themselves. We understand how obvious and redundant this sounds. We also know that there remains great strain between teachers and students across this nation. Only a deep examination of one's own skills and the identification of the most valuable skills to teach students can hope to bridge this gap. We cannot assume that we can effortlessly communicate in the "language of the oppressor" without reevaluating the degree to which we honor the communication styles of our students.

The capacity to communicate has moved from survival purposes to connection purposes. It has allowed for a deepening of bonding in human populations. This is true historically, and it is true today. When a student feels a teacher's authenticity, the lines of communication can be forged and may remain open. Trust, as we will discuss in the next chapter, is born in these open lines.

Reflective Activities

- ◆ Consider the following questions:
    - Has a student (or any person) ever identified something that you have said as offensive? How did you react? How did you feel? How do you think they felt?

    _____
    _____

    - Looking back, how do you wish you had reacted?

    _____
    _____

- ◆ Ask a trusted loved one about a time in which there was obvious dissonance between the contents of your spoken words and your tone or body language. What did you communicate in that moment? What did you want to communicate?

    _____
    _____

- ◆ Determine your preferred communication styles, your communication strengths, and areas to grow. You may need to ask a trusted colleague or friend to help you identify these strengths and areas for growth.

    _____
    _____

- ◆ Consider the following questions with respect to your assessment of students:
    - How do you assess students' writing style? How do you explicitly or implicitly communicate your valuing or devaluing of students' languages and dialects?

    _____
    _____

    - Do you assess students' speaking style? How? Why?

    _____
    _____

- ◆ Identify ways in which you implicitly or explicitly teach your students of the importance of language.

    _____
    _____

References

Alim, H. S., Rickford, J. R., & Ball, A. F. (Eds.). (2016). *Raciolinguistics: How language shapes our ideas about race*. New York: Oxford University Press.

American Psychological Association. (2022). *Bias-free language*. https://apastyle.apa.org/style-grammar-guidelines/bias-free-language/

Centers for Disease Control and Prevention. (2022). *Preferred terms for select population groups & communities*. https://www.cdc.gov/healthcommunication/Preferred_Terms.html

College Board. (2014). *AP® United States History 2014 scoring guidelines*. https://secure-media.collegeboard.org/digitalServices/pdf/ap/ap14_us%20history_scoring_guidelines.pdf

hooks, b. (1994). *Teaching to transgress: Education as the practice of freedom*. London: Routledge.

Paris, D. (2012). Culturally sustaining pedagogy: A needed change in stance, terminology, and practice. *Educational Researcher, 41*, 93. https://doi.org/10.3102/0013189X12441244

Rodgers, C. R., & Raider-Roth, M. B. (2006). Presence in teaching. *Teachers and Teaching: Theory and Practice, 12*, 265–287. https://doi.org/10.1080/13450600500467548

3

Building Trust

How Intentional Vulnerability and Consistency Cultivate Connectedness

Trust is one of the most important goals in the classroom. It is a requirement for forming any meaningful relationship. Breaches of trust result in profound breaks in relationships, both in and outside the field of education, that are difficult to repair. Countless books have been written about trust in romantic relationships, and childhood breaks in trust can result in lifelong damage. Trust is necessary in all successful relationships in our lives; our relationships in the classroom are no different.

We may underestimate the importance of trust since "much of the relevant computations are automatic and take place outside of awareness," but in reality "the human mind constantly tries to ascertain the trustworthiness of others" (DeSteno, 2015, p. xv). When calling attention to these thought processes, it becomes easier to see how often each day we try to determine trustworthiness. We need to determine how much to trust other drivers on the road, the engineers of the stoplights, the teachers and security at our children's schools, our bosses and coworkers, the businesses from which we buy items, and the reviewers who review those items for online purchases – the list can go on and on.

If we take the example of buying an item online – let's say a set of Legos – we can recognize the importance of authenticity in order to trust the seller enough to make the purchase. We might look for the Lego brand, since we are familiar with the quality already, and may scan the item details and photos to ensure that the item is, in fact, what we believe it is. To further authenticate the item, we may already be purchasing from a known store rather than an unknown buyer on eBay, Etsy, or Amazon. We might also notice how language plays a role in our decisions. We might read the details, maybe the number of pieces, and match them up with the item details in the photo. We might also notice if there are significant grammatical errors in the description and that may impact our decision whether or not to trust the seller.

This thought process of using authenticity and language as ways to gauge trustworthiness – as a foundation to trust – is also true in relationships. While most relationships begin as transactional interactions, as experiences accrue, memory builds a schema of shared time spent and the bond has the opportunity to grow. Trust is what allows for this mutual growth to continue.

Assessing How Trust *Feels*

Menakem (2017), in his book *My Grandmother's Hands: Racialized Trauma and the Pathway to Mending Our Hearts and Bodies*, describes a way for us to reveal our emotional and physical responses to those we trust as opposed to those we do not. In the following exercise, we have adapted a "body practice," as Menakem calls it, to demonstrate its value. We encourage you to complete this exercise or, at the very least, begin to notice your feelings in the presence of different people and the degree to which you trust them.

Begin by getting into a comfortable position and closing your eyes. Sit quietly for about a minute, noticing your breath and your surroundings. Now, envision a person you trust walking toward you. Take a moment to identify your emotions. Does your body have any physical reactions (e.g. relaxing of your muscles, a smile beginning to form on your face)?

Now, imagine that person walking away and another person, one whom you do not trust, walking toward you. What emotions do you feel now? What physical changes do you notice in your body?

As Menakem then suggests:

Gently, one by one, feel into all the places in your body where you sense constriction.

Let your attention rest briefly in each one.

Now send the [person you do not trust] away. Bring back the [person you trust]. For several breaths, relax in the safety this presence provides.

Now, gently, move your attention through your body, from your head to your toes, one more time. Feel into each spot where you sense softness. Stay with each of these for one to two seconds.

(p. 32)

A simple activity like this can be a powerful reminder of our emotional and physical responses – our feelings of safety – in the presence (or imagined presence) of a person whom we either trust or distrust. The differences are real and can be distinctly felt. Students, regardless of whether they are aware of it, will not be able to learn most effectively if they feel the discomfort associated with distrust and the accompanying bodily responses. So, while time is needed for trust to build, we need to be committed to the process.

Factors That Contribute to Trust-Building in the Classroom

For some students, particularly those who have been impacted by breaches of trust with others in their lives, it may take more time to build trust and connection. However, the presentation of oneself as an adult who can be trusted, as one who is open and vulnerable and full of love, is key. We wholeheartedly disagree with the "don't smile until Christmas" advice traditionally given to teachers as a way to instill fear (and somehow respect?) in students. With the exception of those who have naturally cold and distant dispositions, those who we imagine are unlikely to choose teaching as a profession, this "advice" will have the opposite impact as intended. Some students, including those who would be engaged regardless of the teacher's personality type, will likely notice at some point in the year that the teacher is inauthentic and will lose trust in the teacher. This will likely result in a superficial working relationship rather than a meaningful connection. Others will initially shut down, as they will perceive the teacher's disposition as uncaring or lacking respect for them. Val fell into the latter group as a student, only trusting teachers whom she felt were honest and truly cared about students. These were also the only teachers with whom she was honest and shared difficulties she was experiencing, whether in the classroom or in her personal life.

VK: I have had many conversations with students who have expressed distrust in teachers, some of whom even believed that *all* teachers couldn't be trusted because their actions in the classroom were merely to keep their jobs. One of these conversations was with one of my most creative-thinking students, someone who also consistently received D and F grades on his report card. He explained that he had teachers that he liked before, but none that he really trusted. He found that he generally began the year with good student-teacher relationships but that they began to deteriorate when he didn't turn in assignments. Not only had his teachers considered this behavior to be "lazy," but they also contacted home before talking with him about the behaviors that they found to be unacceptable.

If these teachers had spoken with *him*, they would have realized that he needed to find personal importance in assignments before he could find them worthy of his time. He did not want to waste time on work that he felt was "busy work": assignments that were given to fill time and had no importance to real life. The choice to call his parents before having a discussion with him was perceived as disrespectful and an act of control rather than a genuine effort to help him succeed. What seemed like "conditional caring" to him resulted in his inability to trust and truly connect with his teachers.

This anecdote also brings up the importance of transparency in building trust. Each of us in our careers independently came to the realization that explaining the justifications for our actions and lesson choices led to positive outcomes in the classroom. While we may not have initially recognized that we were building trust by doing this, we were demonstrating that our choices in the classroom had meaning. They were not simply to control students into compliance and check off the boxes to maintain our employment.

This experience also recognizes the importance of dependability and consistency in caring. Educators shouldn't only demonstrate care when a student is "behaving." Our care for students should be clear regardless of their choices, and this is the only way that trust can be built. We look for such unconditional and reliable support in our adult relationships too, as ways to build, or break, trust.

Brown (2017) uses the acronym BRAVING to discuss what she has determined to be the seven elements of trust – Boundaries, Reliability, Accountability, Vault, Integrity, Nonjudgment, and Generosity. Her research shows that trust is built in small moments that can serve as either opportunities to build trust or opportunities to betray another.

We want to highlight two of these elements – "vault" and "nonjudgment" – as they relate to student-teacher relationships (STRs). Serving as a "vault" for another – allowing them to know that their personal information is safe – is something we also value; however, in the classroom this can become difficult in terms of professional boundaries and safety. So, while being a "vault" is something we both find to be essential in our adult relationships, we come back to the importance of transparency here. Each of us has had experiences where students have shared information that may have impacted their safety, and, as a result, we needed to contact their counselors. In each of these cases, we knew that the students had trusted us in sharing such information and feared the potential breaking of that trust by sharing their personal information. However, recognizing how transparency can serve as another way to build trust, we shared *why* we needed to share the information and how we planned to do so. In most cases, we also accompanied the student to guidance to serve as further support. Serving as a "vault" for another undoubtedly has value, but in the field of education, since our primary purpose is keeping children safe, our first priority is transparency. After all, as teachers, we are *in loco parentis* and we cannot serve in the same capacity as a trusted friend.

We also acknowledge "nonjudgment" to be an important part of trust-building, but we have found that the best way to convey this to students, in a dynamic where we will be consistently providing feedback, is by helping students embrace a growth mindset. (We will discuss developing a growth mindset in greater detail in Chapter 6.) We recognize that students may feel "judged" by our constructive feedback, as we can feel "judged" by theirs. However, if we know that this is rooted in a place of caring and that the ultimate goal is growth, then the feeling of judgment will give rise to shared progress. So, while maintaining "nonjudgment" may be a more difficult element to achieve in the classroom, we can reframe – through the use of explicit language! – this concept in a way that also helps to build trust. We would reframe "judgment" as kind truth-telling in the form of objective evaluation rather than assigning moral value to it.

Finding points of connection with a student, as we will discuss more in later chapters, also plays a role in developing trust. DeSteno (2015) has found that a child's ability to relate to an adult contributes significantly to their decision to trust them. As a result, he suggests that educators:

> have to pay attention not only to ways to maximize their competence and intellectual authority, but also to ways to identify links to young students. A teacher may not speak with an accent similar to that of a new pupil, but if he or she lives in the same neighborhood, has the same kind of pet, or experienced a similar past challenge as the student, highlighting this fact will allow a link of association to be made.
>
> (p. 77)

Impacts of Trusting Relationships

From *The Body Keeps the Score*, we learn that "secure attachment develops when caregiving includes emotional attunement," and this is an excellent reminder that, as teachers, we want to be constantly striving for secure attachment to our students (van der Kolk, 2015, p. 113). Kate refers to this relationship as the

STR and she shares with her students in September that this relationship will be grounded in trust and communication. But this foundation doesn't exist until teachers and students alike go through time together and spend hours in the classroom learning and teaching. Once they are engaged in mutual work and they begin to feel emotions on a regular basis in shared time and space, trust grows. One of Kate's students recently recognized that they trusted her more once they got to know her through the dynamic of the class. This student recognized how the shared time and Kate's explicit discussions of the importance of trust contributed to the meaningful development of the STR. As this trust grows, empathy increases, which also has the capacity to deepen trust further.

KMH: When I was a child, and there was truth to what a person said to me, I felt honored and seen. I vow to earn my students' trust, and be worthy of it, and be a truth-teller, too. We entrust into the hands and hearts of our students our own truth at great risk. Our students, too, in ways they cannot even know, need us to be those they can trust the most.

Beyond relationship-building, research has shown that trust in an educator also plays a role in a student's ability to learn, particularly in their encoding and consolidating new knowledge. As DeSteno (2014) notes, "At heart, learning often comes down to believing you can trust what you are told, and by as early as three years of age our minds are already categorizing informants – parents included – as trustworthy or not" (p. 76).

Additionally, research has found trust to be an important predictor of both student commitment (or "buy-in") and engagement (Cavanagh et al., 2018; Wang et al., 2021). In fact, Cavanagh et al. (2018) found trust in an instructor to be a stronger predictor of student outcomes, measured by commitment, engagement, and final grade, than growth mindset. Wang et al. (2021) confirmed that, while both play important roles in increasing student buy-in, trust was a stronger and more consistent predictor of positive student outcomes than growth mindset. So, serving as a trusted adult for students helps them to better retain information provided *and* engage with such information, necessary aspects for the learning process.

The Importance of Trust Schoolwide

While we may have the most control over the student-teacher trust bond, in order for the most positive outcomes, other trusting relationships come into play. For example, students learning to navigate trust with peers, counselors, and administrators are critical life skills. In order for trust to grow, relationships need to be established, and opportunities need to be provided for each of these types of connections to build. Ideally, class size and counselor-student and administrator-student ratios would be low enough for these opportunities to be more personal. However, we recognize the systemic challenges that exist and prevent these situations from occurring. Therefore, counselors and administrators need to make greater efforts to interact and build relationships rooted in trust. Vulnerability and transparency, again, play important roles in these processes, as these can be the keys to unlocking meaningful connections.

Educators, too, seek trusting relationships with administrators. We have found that the greatest source of trust-building with administrators has resulted from administrator transparency. For example, when we, as teachers, are told to complete tasks – especially those that we may not initially support or understand – we want to know the justification for them. We want to know that our time is being valued and put toward a meaningful goal, ideally a shared one. A lack of transparency can be damaging to an effective working relationship or can prevent one from starting in the first place.

A teacher-administrator relationship should effectively reflect the STR – it should be a partnership in learning and growth. We hope that administrators at any level recognize that our writing in this book applies in all of the topics we explore, as the administrator becomes the "teacher" and the teacher becomes the "student."

Although it may seem daunting to develop trusting relationships with everyone in your workplace, simple actions can prove effective. For example, Zak (2017) acknowledges that leaders in high-trust workplaces engage in joint decision-making with colleagues. Since these actions produce oxytocin, they increase trust and cooperation levels in the workplace. This, too, applies to the classroom and teacher-student relationship, as we will discuss increasing student choice and voice later in the book. Such intentional actions can offer vulnerability and set the tone for effective and meaningful relationships.

To sum up, trust is essential in relationship-building and community-building. It is a prerequisite to creating and nurturing emotional safety. We have isolated it in this chapter to signify the necessity of cultivating trust in the field of education and will continue to come back to its importance in the next chapters.

Reflective Activities

- Identify the characteristics of a person you trust. Do you exhibit these qualities in the classroom?
  _____
  _____
  _____

- Consider your own personality type. How does that impact the way in which you connect to others?
  _____
  _____
  _____

- Consider whether you have any past issues with trust and how this may impact your relationships in your educational role.
  _____
  _____
  _____

- Create a list of activities that may be effective in your role to build trust with students. Set a short-term goal to complete one of these activities.
  _____
  _____
  _____

References

Brown, B. (2017). *Braving the wilderness: The quest for true belonging and the courage to stand alone* (1st ed.). New York: Random House.

Cavanagh, A. J., Chen, X., Bathgate, M., Frederick, J., Hanauer, D. I., & Graham, M. J. (2018). Trust, growth mindset, and student commitment to active learning in a college science course. *CBE Life Sciences Education, 17*(1), ar10. https://doi.org/10.1187/cbe.17-06-0107

DeSteno, D. (2015). *The truth about trust: How it determines success in life, love, learning, and more.* New York: Plume.

Menakem, R. (2017). *My grandmother's hands: Racialized trauma and the pathway to mending our hearts and bodies.* Las Vegas, NV: Central Recovery Press.

van der Kolk, B. A. (2015). *The body keeps the score: Brain, mind, and body in the healing of trauma.* New York: Penguin Books.

Wang, C., Cavanagh, A. J., Bauer, M., Reeves, P. M., Gill, J. C., Chen, X., Hanauer, D. I., & Graham, M. J. (2021). *A framework of college student buy-in to evidence-based teaching practices in STEM: The roles of trust and growth mindset.* https://doi.org/10.1187/cbe.20-08-0185

Zak, P. J. (2017). The neuroscience of trust. *Harvard Business Review.* January–February, 84–90.

4

Creating and Nurturing Emotional Safety

How a Safe and Supportive Classroom Fosters Student Growth, Learning, and Empowerment

We recognize that emotional safety is a necessary component of a successful learning environment and that it takes much labor to both create and sustain this in a classroom full of young people with diverse backgrounds and needs. Trust, as we have already discussed, and respect, which we will discuss now, are essential to the creation of emotional safety. Sustaining and nurturing feelings of emotional safety in each student, as well as the teacher, depend upon practices that promote caring, community building, and vulnerability.

Respect in the Classroom

We define respect as the way a person treats another human that shows that they are worthy and that they are being held in high regard. This can be communicated through our actions, words, attention, and time provided for an individual's needs. Our choices, and the students' choices, demonstrate respect or its absence, and this greatly impacts the classroom climate.

Some students will come to the classroom with a preconceived degree of respect and a blind trust for their teacher, and others will come to the classroom with no expectation, believing that their teachers will need to earn their respect and trust. We cannot expect each student to blindly trust and respect us, as each student enters our classrooms with different life experiences. For certain students, a feeling of safety in the classroom may not come right away.

However, we need to be committed to gaining their respect, since the respect of all students is necessary to have a classroom community based on emotional safety. As we have discussed already, doing one's best to be authentic and empathetic with the students will help to build student connections anchored in respect and trust.

VK: "You don't respect me, so why should I respect you?"

    I remember hearing a student say this to a teacher in high school and hearing it numerous times, luckily not directed at me, during my teaching career. I also remember feeling this way as a teenage student, not wanting to engage in positive ways with teachers who seemed not to care about me as an individual. I didn't recognize it at the time, but I realize now that I needed the teacher to extend kindness *first*. I have always been the type to observe before engaging with another person, and I use that observation period to determine whether or not I will extend trust.

    When hearing that question, I always cringed. It was spoken as a challenge to a teacher and sometimes ended in an ego-led attempt on the part of the teacher to demonstrate dominance. This would always end badly. Alternately, this challenge could have been, but rarely was, treated as an opportunity to begin establishing rapport rooted in mutual respect. Looking back, the students I heard say this to teachers were those who really *did* want to build a meaningful relationship. These were students who did not necessarily have many positive relationships with adults in their lives and also lacked the courage to be vulnerable in offering respect to their teacher first. It was crushing to witness this open-hearted vulnerability on the part of a teenager be met with such unwillingness to uncover the true motivations of the student.

While certainly we will grow to admire our students more as we learn their specific qualities and strengths, we suggest educators arrive with and maintain a high regard for each student, rather than insisting they earn it from us. Students have many competing pressures throughout the school day, and feeling they need to prove themselves to the teacher likely will prevent them from feeling secure in a classroom. If we really want to create and build emotional safety, we need to be vulnerable and extend our respect and trust to students upon meeting them. We acknowledge that, at some point, our students may act in ways that test *our* depth of respect and trust in them. But, if we are to truly *teach* them, we also need to provide opportunities to repair any breach, as well as discussion and reflection of what has occurred.

It may be a more difficult task to ensure that students respect each other, yet this is another necessary component to building an environment where students are safe to be themselves. However, there are numerous ways to encourage and promote trust and respect in the classroom. Explicit discussions of the importance of respect on the first days of school and repeated in the months thereafter are a good first step. We may want to utilize the walls in our classrooms to display reminders of the importance of respect and refer to them as needed. We may want to assign qualities of character for students to embody and encourage in others, as Kate discusses later. We may want to plan lesson tasks that encourage genuine conversation among students, allowing space for connectedness and relatability. It is important that these discussions and activities are genuine and authentic for each educator, so they will likely look different in every setting.

The Importance of Emotional Safety

Students often don't think about the dynamics of relationship in the classroom unless someone calls attention to them. They often don't consider the active relationship-building that needs to occur with the teacher and their peers, being more familiar with their "relationships" outside of the school day with family and friends. As a result, it is the responsibility of the teacher to be explicit in reminding students that their actions and language in the classroom each day contribute to the building or deterioration of such relationships. In order to feel comfortable establishing and sustaining these relationships within the classroom, each person needs to feel emotionally safe.

Emotional safety, for us, means comfortability in vulnerability and risk-taking, and unconditional support and caring, even when mistakes are made. It must be something that our students see *in* us and feel *from* us. It must radiate out that we serve a "place" of emotional safety until the students can learn to provide it for themselves.

Relationships in which we feel emotional safety allow us to speak our truth and be our authentic selves, serving as psychological sanctuary. People who allow us to feel safe include family members, especially our mamas. Jo Ann and Barbara are two amazing women who raised us and served as our sources of stability and emotional safety. They provided emotional safety by being people we knew would always behave the same way and love us unconditionally. In raising us and our siblings, they were predictable, kind, loving, and caring. They defended us against threats, listened to us, praised us as we needed, and made us feel worthy. We could feel their pride in us as we grew into the women they knew we would become. They always saw the best in us, looking past our temporary failings and showing us love in each moment of our lives.

Because we were shown these role models, we are able to embody this degree of caring in our teaching and mothering lives. Regardless of whether we are related to someone, we know what it means to "be there" for another person. It means to be fully present as a tender, gentle, supportive, loving person.

Each of us has also had people in our lives turn on us, and we know how that feels too. Those relationships do *not* feel safe, even when there are no active problems occurring. Though some individuals will thrive in spite of this lack of safety, often their growth is impeded when they do not feel safe in the relationships in that environment. We need to ensure, to the extent that we are able, that our classrooms are free from the threat of emotional discomfort and stress.

Emotional safety is something we human beings crave and cherish when we find it in relationships with others. It serves as a source of stability and provides a space for growth. We, Val and Kate, did find what we call psychological sanctuary in one another. One of us was more guarded, and one of us was more trusting, yet we were able to cultivate a friendship as fellow teachers that was rooted in hope and optimism. Through our courage, we were able to discern that our alliance was healthy and good for us and for our professional lives. A rare type of friendship, there is nothing in life we cannot discuss. We discuss boundaries, too, and happily seek one another's advice on creating them where they are necessary or important.

We find emotional safety with a select group of friends and with our life partners and children. We do not place emotional burdens upon our children that they cannot handle, but we do let our children see the range of our emotions. While it would not be true to declare ourselves entirely and perfectly emotionally healthy, we can safely assert that we have each done a great deal of emotional work to be able to be people who cultivate emotional safety in our own personal and professional lives. This process is an active, energetic, and ongoing one that we continue to refine. As Val is cleaning poop off her son's hand and Kate's son is yelling at the piano as he teaches himself to play "Jingle Bells" in August, we are fully present for one another, fully accepting of one another, fully seeing one another as we need to be seen. This is the gift of emotional safety. In her book *All About Love* (2000), hooks says, "rarely, if ever, are any of us healed in isolation. Healing is an act of communion" (p. 215). We are in communion as we heal one another through friendship; we are in communion as we write this book.

Emotional safety is requisite for being a whole human. Otherwise, we hold back, hold in, close up, and turn inward. Emotional safety, as identified and held up as fundamentally important by the teacher, provides a means for keeping hearts and brains open. And a classroom where hearts can be safely opened is a place where we all can grow.

Essentially, there is no point in developing effective lessons if we cannot create a classroom environment in which students can feel safe enough to focus (more on that when we discuss stress). We are reminded through Maslow's hierarchy that meeting students' need for safety allows for the possibility to develop feelings of belongingness, self-esteem, and self-actualization, all of which we want to cultivate in our students.

Strategies to Cultivate Emotional Safety in the Classroom

The use of the term "safe space" in academic contexts has suggested understanding of the importance of feelings of safety in the classroom. In recent years, some educators have favored establishing a "brave space" in which students can challenge and be challenged in a supportive environment (Arao & Clemens, 2013). While a completely safe environment cannot be promised, as no one can predict what may arise, and a brave environment may be emotionally taxing, especially for those from historically marginalized groups, the *commitment* to providing safety and valuing bravery, accountability, and growth is what students need. We do our best to make this commitment clear to students on the first day of class and throughout the year, especially when difficult topics arise. Val has had students also commit and sign their agreement as a promise to make the classroom a safe place for others and to be brave in facing difficult topics, reminding them that growth is the goal for everyone, herself included. She also has asked students to commit to genuine efforts at "calling in" rather than "calling out" their peers and teachers, appreciating individual perspectives, and respecting the bravery of those who share aloud regardless of agreement or relatability.

While one may believe that avoiding difficult topics in class will result in feelings of emotional safety, we argue that a supportive classroom should instead face these topics with care and support and recognize and respond to student issues as they arise. As a history educator, Val appreciates the desire to teach tragedies and injustices with the appropriate gravity and care. History must be faced with courage so that, as Angelou (1993) noted, it "need not be lived again." But we also need to be mindful of our own lived experiences and how they impact our choice of content and our manner of teaching it. We need to listen to our students when they express discomfort based on their experiences. In a memorable example, one of Val's Black students, while watching an episode of *Eyes on the Prize* to learn about the Civil Rights

Movement, said, "Miss, I don't want to watch Black people getting beat up." She chose to honor his discomfort, and instead of requiring him to watch the film, they had a meaningful discussion about the contents of the documentary and his own personal connections to it.

We can, with courage, discuss with students what may be triggering and the ways in which we can best address such discomfort. In Val's experience, some useful strategies that have come from these conversations have included providing lesson previews to alert students to potentially difficult content ahead of time, allowing students to write reflections in place of the triggering activity, and providing students with content readings in place of visual material. Additionally, we should take an inventory of our content to ensure that the experiences of historically marginalized groups are not erased and that joys are balanced with injustices. Doing so is also a way of providing emotional safety for students, helping them to feel seen and valued in a nonverbal, yet still explicit, manner.

As teachers, we also need to actively establish and maintain connections with students, especially those who represent backgrounds and identity groups different from our own, as these are the students who are more likely to question whether we truly understand them. Students need to know that their teachers care about and value them as humans as well as learners. This is the key to building communities of empowerment. Even seemingly simple acts, like Kate's recent decision to take class time for students to share photos of the Junior Prom, can demonstrate this care. The sharing of something meaningful and special that made the students all so happy was one means of fostering the emotional safety of the class and celebrating the students as *whole* humans.

In order to allow each student, as well as each teacher, to feel comfortable being themselves, every individual needs to feel that they can be understood. While it may be more difficult to foster these truly empathetic relationships among students, it is especially vital in student-teacher relationships. Students are very perceptive to a lack of teacher connection, or, more importantly, the *perceived* lack of teacher connection. Each of us has heard stories from students who felt that their teacher "hated" them. Some of the most common justifications they used as evidence included:

- not knowing the student's name
- repeatedly mispronouncing the student's name
- not remembering something the student had previously told them
- "giving" the student a bad grade with little feedback
- never asking the student about their lives
- not looking the student in the eye

- mentioning the holidays of other students but not those they celebrate
- doling out seemingly unprovoked or disproportionate punishment
- not allowing the student to explain themselves when accused of a misbehavior
- showing favoritism toward other students

It is important to note that teachers may not be deliberately engaging in any of these behaviors, but the students experienced these as the teacher's inability to understand them as people, which resulted in the students' putting up walls as a defensive measure.

Students will not only have difficulty connecting with the teacher but will likely also lose engagement in content and motivation. This is particularly important for students of color, who may feel disconnected from or misunderstood by white teachers, which is worth acknowledging, as both represent the majority of their respective groups (Seider & Graves, 2020). If a teacher is accused of any of these or similar behaviors or recognizes them in themselves, the best course of action is to validate the student and apologize. Again, the show of vulnerability can only help to repair the breach of trust that occurred.

As often as possible, we publicly acknowledge mistakes to model that while mistakes may bring shame, this negative feeling can be transmuted into learning and personal growth. We apologize to the students when we feel we have not done our best – whether we didn't know the answer to their question, didn't fully listen to them or acknowledge their contribution, or even were ourselves late to class on a given day. This demonstration of empathy and desire for improvement shows the students that we care in our efforts to build relationship and community.

The Importance of Empathy in the Classroom

Framing teaching as an act of caring, which we believe it is – for the individual, for the class, for the school community, for society at large – requires that we keep empathy at the forefront. Empathy is commonly understood as the understanding and sharing of the feelings of another. This sharing of feelings, and the physical reactions that accompany them, is possible because of mirror neurons. Mirror neurons in the prefrontal cortex of the brain enable us to unconsciously react to our environment and respond to the actions and emotions of others. Rizzolatti and Craighero (2005) explain, "When we observe others, we enact their actions inside ourselves and we share their emotions" (p. 119).

True empathy, however, goes beyond reflecting another's emotional response and requires leaning into one's own self-awareness. This deep experience of empathy is recognizing your own emotions, holding those as true, and seeing in the other their own emotion, which may be a completely *different* set of emotions than yours. Brown (2021) clarifies the meaning of empathy when she writes, "Rather than walking in your shoes, I need to learn how to listen to the story you tell about what it's like in your shoes *and* believe you even when it doesn't match my experiences" (p. 123).

Recognizing your level of self-awareness in regard to how you experience empathy must be a high priority. This recognition may be the result of a trial-and-error process throughout our teaching careers and lives. We educators are in a profession in which our empathy is constantly tested, giving us the gift of growth in our capacity for empathy. For some, empathy comes as naturally as breathing and may need less practice. For others, it will take effort to actively remind oneself to read the emotions and try to understand the experiences of those with whom we interact. As an example, if a student is late to class and immediately asks to go to the bathroom, how do we react? Do we experience anger, as they have interrupted class, or do we recognize the strain and embarrassment on their face suggesting they may be having stomach troubles?

Interacting in an empathetic way is a decision that can undoubtedly better our relationships and teaching. It is an active choice to look at the facial expressions and body language of other people, to gather data about others' emotions, and then to decide whether and how to respond to what we have observed. Many may avoid this choice to engage in active empathy because it will require emotional energy and time. This degree of emotional investment and responsiveness can make a lasting impression on not just the student who was directly in question but every other student witnessing an encounter. We learn so very much from how someone is treated by a teacher, even when we ourselves are simply the observers.

An authentically caring teacher has a deep well of empathy and calls upon it moment to moment while orchestrating the day in and day out tasks of running a classroom. Demonstrations of care do not need to be large to be felt. Care is shown in our responses to students who are late to class, whether we choose to allow students to make up work, and even our choice to pick up a pen that has fallen from a student's desk.

Caring relationships, in which empathy is at the forefront, ideally represent all the relationships between adults and students in a school building. A caring relationship should be recognized as such by recipients of the care, and if it is not, we would suggest reflection and feedback to determine the reason. As Noddings (2013) writes, "Whatever [one] does for the cared-for is embedded in a relationship that reveals itself as engrossment and in an attitude that warms and comforts the cared-for" (p. 19). It is only in the presence of a "one-caring" who fosters an environment of emotional safety that the student-teacher relationship can grow.

This caring, not only by teachers but others who hold power – administrators, school board, and even the government – can be communicated in various ways, including the availability of resources and the physical appearance of a classroom or school building (Rolón-Dow, 2005). While individual educators may lack control over these factors, it can be meaningful to recognize systemic inequities to validate students' experiences. This can serve as a way to understand students more deeply. Increasing this depth of understanding of one's students is especially necessary in cases where the teacher may be seen as an "outsider." This can also be an opportunity to demonstrate caring regarding the issues – big and small – that impact the daily lives of our students. Rolón-Dow (2005) notes that a "color(full) critical care praxis" is one that "begins by acknowledging that, to care for students of color in the United States, we must seek to understand the role that race/ethnicity has played in shaping and defining the sociocultural and political conditions of their communities." This means, for example, acknowledging that an educator's own race and ethnicity may be tied to privilege and advantage in ways that may differ from those of their students. We agree with Rolón-Dow that "educators thus need to care enough to understand how such issues as White privilege and racism, colonization, migration, and citizenship have played out in the communities where they teach" (p. 104).

Standing with students on these issues and taking action to show our care of the students and their communities demonstrates genuine effort and allows for trust-building. Here, again, we acknowledge the importance of self-awareness and self-reflection on the part of the educator. Rather than caring for a person in the way *we* want to be cared for, we should care for them in the way *they* want to be cared for, as our experiences do not necessarily represent those of our students. In order to best learn how our students need to be cared for, we must think carefully about the right questions to ask and then *listen*.

The Importance of Listening in the Classroom

A key skill in creating and nurturing emotional safety in a classroom, or anywhere else, is listening. Nhất Hạnh (2001/2009) writes about the skill of "deep listening" as an "art we must cultivate" (p. 61). Before creating and cultivating a classroom climate where everyone feels comfortable, safe, and heard, we must practice listening and truly become exceptional listeners, first to ourselves and then to other human beings:

> First you have to be able to listen to yourself before you can listen to someone else. You must not run away from yourself, but rather be very compassionate toward yourself. The practice of mindfulness will generate the compassion you need to cradle your own pain and suffering. Then, when you begin to understand and love yourself, you are ready to understand and love another person.
> (Nhất Hạnh, 2001/2009, p. 61)

While the educative process does indeed require critical thinking at its core, before anyone will want to hear the suggestion of a teacher, they will want to know they are safe to try and safe to fail. Thus, a teacher who can convey compassion through the skill of deep listening will create a space that does just this. Nhất Hạnh says, "You do not listen in order to judge, criticize, or evaluate. You listen for one reason alone: to offer that person a chance to express [themself]" (p. 62).

How can we make our classroom a place where compassionate listening and critical listening can coexist? First, we learn to listen with all of our heart. Listening can be an act of love. When someone listens to another, it allows them to feel heard, seen, and even loved. When we listen to our students with care and understanding, we teach them to do the same. We can model for our students the ability to listen with open-heartedness and a willingness to be questioned. Kate reminds her students often, "If anything the teacher says or does makes you feel uncomfortable or less safe in any way, then you speak up."

Listening, as an act of love, is also a form of validation, a way of honoring a person's experience. Validating students through listening can serve as a way to build confidence and motivate further participation in the class. Everyone wants to know that their thoughts are valued, and the most basic form of showing that someone's words have value is through active listening. Active listening, or exhibiting simultaneous verbal and nonverbal signals of attention and understanding, is necessary to ensure a supportive classroom dynamic in which meaningful connections can form and flourish. Listening fully and actively, with the aim of truly understanding another, also requires open-mindedness. Garrison (1996), in "A Deweyan Theory of Democratic Listening," reminds us, "Remaining open is awkward. We must be willing to live with confusion and uncertainty about both ourselves and the other person we are attempting to understand. Openness involves risk and vulnerability, but that is how we grow" (p. 433).

Active and open listening is of particular importance when building connections with students of identity groups different from our own. These students, likely knowing that you do not identify in one or more of the ways that they do, may be hesitant to even share their experiences, especially if they have previously felt dismissed by others outside of their identity groups.

We also can and should help students build their listening skills in order to strengthen their classroom relationships. Students should be explicitly taught how to listen and how to show that they are listening. We might ask students to illustrate what it looks like to listen or not listen, or to describe what it feels like to be heard or unheard. Activities that require input from peers should also be utilized frequently in the classroom. Answering student-created discussion questions, using the knowledge of a peer to build a response, or summarizing responses before offering their own not only builds listening skills but also can build content knowledge and create a sense of community that capitalizes on the strengths of all members. Asking students to demonstrate listening in our conversations with them can also be useful. We might ask students to reflect on what they heard in teacher feedback or to summarize content or instructions. These intentional choices to check in can be helpful in building listening skills, identifying areas to improve, and clarifying areas of misconception.

The benefits of listening are numerous. Garrison (1996) says, "Listening cultivates growth." In terms of personal growth, we can "[create] new understandings among people, and this implies a willingness to change one's own understanding and ways of being in the face of new challenges and insights" (p. 446). Beyond this personal growth, listening promotes growth in relationships, building feelings of trust, which can translate to feelings of safety.

It is also important to listen with particular attention to student needs. Collecting individual feedback from students, which we will discuss more fully in the next chapter, is a further way to show that we are listening. Giving students a greater voice, and actually listening to these voices, can help us determine whether student needs are being met. This might mean, for example, asking pointed questions in a more private or even anonymous setting to allow students to feel comfortable sharing honestly. As Wilson (2002) writes, "There are times when it is to our benefit to pay close attention to what others think of us and to consider revising our self-views accordingly, even if this means adopting a more negative view of ourselves" (p. 199). It is not that we suggest we feel bad about ourselves, but rather that we step into a way of seeing ourselves through the eyes of our students that allows us to make useful adjustments in our habitual classroom behavior. More important than whether the feedback is positive or negative is the act of soliciting it in the first place.

Utilizing Trauma-Sensitive Practices

Responding to student needs becomes especially important in cases of traumatic events. A student shared with Val after the death of another student who was a close friend that the absence of acknowledgment by a teacher made her feel that the life of the person did not matter to that teacher. While this may not have been intentional – maybe it served a way to protect the teacher's own mental health – awareness, practice, and transparency need to be considered in these instances. As responsive educators, we need to acknowledge the event and the feelings – the fear, the sadness, the frustration, the grief – and how it will impact the students in the immediate aftermath as well as the long-term impacts.

Ignoring traumatic events, especially those experienced more deeply by cultural or racial groups different from our own, will likely result in a significant disconnect with students from that group, as students have shared that it makes them feel invisible and assume that their teacher has no understanding of their life experiences. This is not to say that we need to relive trauma with the students, especially if we are also grieving or experiencing the trauma alongside them, but the event must be acknowledged and space should be provided for students if it is needed. It might help to write down *our* feelings and messages for our students. Val prepared a speech to share with students at the beginning of class following the death of a student, allowing her to reflect on her own thoughts and giving her a point of focus in case her emotions took over. When her emotions did take over, she paused and was still able to express everything that she felt she needed to say. In taking this step, she was intentional in her attempt to honor the trauma and the loss.

Reflective activities that help students identify what they need during times of difficulty and loss and what they can help provide to others can be very helpful. It allows students the opportunity to express feelings in a more focused way and to support one another. Participating in the activity alongside one's students also shows that the teacher is experiencing the event with them and can help the teacher to process their feelings as well. Val, in participating in a reflective activity alongside her students, was able to hear what they would want others to do for them in a time of loss. She was ultimately able to honor one student's request when he experienced a loss later that year.

It is difficult to know what to say after a tragedy since there is never a "right" thing and so many "wrong" things. (The organization Good Grief has helpful resources to identify these.) It is important to be as intentional as you are able and say *something* so the students know they are not alone.

How to Encourage Emotional Risk-Taking in the Classroom

Just as we need to be open and vulnerable in the classroom to build better connections with students, we want students to practice vulnerability for their own growth and relationship-building. One of the best ways to encourage this is to model it for students and to explicitly discuss the importance of being vulnerable in closing the distance between individuals. As we mentioned in the previous chapter, vulnerability on the part of the educator inspires trust, which is the foundation of a healthy student-teacher relationship, and functions to establish an environment in which openness and emotional risk-taking are valued.

Often when discussing social and emotional learning (SEL) in professional development meetings, teachers groan about how to incorporate such activities into the classroom. Some comment that they "can't just take a day to talk about emotions" or that "this might work in health class but not in science class." To us, these comments seem to suggest a denial of the importance of connection-building in the classroom, essentially a denial of decades of research that prove otherwise. They suggest discomfort on the part of the teacher to engage in the emotional work of teaching and perhaps discomfort to face their own emotional truths. One important purpose of this book is to convince the reader that human emotion and the physical impacts of these emotions must be acknowledged for healthy, meaningful relationships, of any kind, to be built. Ignoring this does a disservice to the teacher, as it makes their work more difficult since their relationships with students and among students will suffer, and, more importantly, a disservice to the students who may not be able to reach their full potential in the classroom without the sense of a supportive and safe learning environment.

We would argue that class time at the beginning of the year must aim to build connections among students and that jumping directly into content without first establishing the goals and the plan to achieve an emotionally safe space, will ultimately be detrimental. While some teachers may want to take full days or large portions of class during the year to establish their classroom connections, others may want to use activities within lessons, or both! Small group discussions around questions such as "What is something you often do not share with people you first meet?" when talking about character interactions in a novel or "What is a problem in your life you recently encountered and how did you attempt to solve it?" when discussing different ways to arrive at a solution in a math class can lead to meaningful learning as well as relationship-building among students.

Addressing Disruptions in the Emotional Safety of the Classroom

We know from our own experiences that there will be times when our efforts to build classroom climate and emotional safety fail. We believe that it is important to recognize these as opportunities for learning and growth and to acknowledge these aloud to the class to rebuild connection. This recognition models openness, vulnerability, and a growth mindset and contributes to an atmosphere where students can feel safe to make mistakes. Every teacher will likely have examples of this, maybe many of them.

Here we each explain experiences in which we failed to ensure emotional safety in the classroom, but we were able to learn valuable lessons as a result of our handling of the situations.

KMH: Many years ago, perhaps ten, I was starting off the school year in what was at that time my "new" way, prioritizing our classroom climate and establishing the way we would interact and treat one another as far and away more important than the subject matter of the course. I was on a *mission*. I was determined to teach my students, within the context of the biology classroom, to be people of integrity. To do this, I enlisted the help of "The Virtues Project," first suggested to me by my sociology professor, Dr. Tanja Sargent. Knowing that the word "virtue" might not be overwhelmingly welcomed by all, I decided to call the activity the "Qualities of Character."

At the time I was going through a divorce, and I was in pain. You can imagine that coming to work each day with a smile on my face and lightness and joy in my heart used up a massive amount of cognitive energy in my teaching life. Determined to keep my personal and professional lives separate, I used compartmentalization as my primary coping mechanism. I was known affectionately at school by one colleague as "Happy Heavers." I did a very, very good job impersonating a happy person. Understandably, going through this difficult transition in life made me emotionally fragile and, at times, harsher in the classroom. As we all know, it is generally harder to be kind when you are suffering.

There was a student who was in tune. There is no other way to explain it. He seemed to have an intuitive sense that I was suffering, though I never revealed anything explicitly about what I was going through. If I slipped and lost tact, this young man would raise his hand and say, "Miss Heavers, that was not a kind thing to say." And so it began that I realized I needed an "Ambassador of Kindness." I appointed him as such, and the rest of the year went better. His presence in my classroom was my reminder to "be kind."

From this experience, I got the idea to assign my students a "Quality of Character" for the year that they would each embody. When we give the language of these qualities to our students – diligence, cooperation, respect, trustworthiness, enthusiasm, courage, justice, courtesy, tact, peacefulness, joyfulness, honesty, self-discipline, flexibility – and ask them to embody them, we are deepening the degree of connection possible within the learning environment through the relationships in the classroom. As part of creating a nurturing space where students can feel and *actually be* emotionally safe, we put the work into the hands of the students themselves. As just one person, it is not physically or emotionally possible to keep all students from harm at all times, as a glance, a look, a word, a raised set of eyebrows, an eye roll, a turning away can all be cause for hurt. As Ricketts (2021) says, trauma can result from "any experience that is distressing or emotionally painful, that overwhelms your ability to cope and leaves you feeling powerless" (p. 97). When we are creating our safe classroom, we are doing so to prevent further trauma.

You will read about self-regulation later on in this book. The focus will be on teaching self-regulation to the students, but it will also include an explanation of just how powerful self-regulation of yourself as a teacher can be. Brown's (2013) "rule" to live by shows us the importance of getting our minds and hearts put right before we enter a classroom. If we do not want our students to incur trauma from our failure to monitor the classroom properly, or worse, from our inability to curtail our own careless comments, we must put sustained effort into our own healing. As Brown says, it is unethical to disclose information about oneself in order to work through one's trauma. She is cautioning here against using your students as free therapists. A heightened self-awareness and practiced full present-moment awareness are what make this possible.

As a result of adopting this activity and incorporating the teaching of character qualities in my classroom, I have empowered students to regulate their own social and emotional interactions with greater self-awareness and intention. More importantly, I have given the students the power to call into question my behaviors as if I were their equal human and not simply a person whose authority can never be called into question. There have been numerous memorable examples in which students have demonstrated the benefit of this activity, using their voices to participate in the creation of an emotionally safe classroom for every member, the teacher included.

VK: When I consider the importance of emotional safety in a classroom, I can't help but be reminded of one class section years ago, where I struggled to provide that for my students, despite my best efforts. In this particular class, there were several students who exhibited attention-seeking behaviors, some of which were received as disrespect aimed toward other classmates. My course was heavily discussion-based, and I quickly found, unsurprisingly, that only the most confident students felt comfortable participating after there had been a few examples of sarcasm and disingenuous contributions from a few of the students. I had private conversations with the individual students, which all resulted in temporary success in the classroom and a corresponding increase in student participation. In an effort to have more sustained success, and really because I was running out of ideas, for the first time in my teaching career, I decided to try a seating chart. I typically allow students to sit in the places in the room where they feel most comfortable and work with them to choose alternate seats if they find that they are unable to focus or achieve success in the seats originally chosen. I was very transparent that the new seating chart was designed to help students connect with others and prevent distraction and disruption as much as possible. I wanted it to be clear that I was trying, even beyond what I thought was best classroom practice, to address the discomfort I saw in the classroom. It backfired.

One of the students had a *very* vocal negative reaction to his new seat, stemming from a prior experience in another classroom in which he felt targeted by the teacher. Unfortunately, I had unknowingly triggered this memory and his subsequent outburst. This led to other students voicing their unhappiness and, luckily, a few looking at me with eyes that told me that they understood. I allowed each unhappy student to voice their frustrations and apologized individually to each. I then apologized to the entire class and explained how I, too, felt frustrated that our classroom climate felt off. My explanation ended with an agreement to return them to their chosen seats after we had experimented for a few days with this arrangement. That honest conversation and the new seating arrangement that prompted it ultimately helped to show students that I prioritized their comfort and that I was trying my best to be responsive to their needs.

While we cannot always provide emotional safety for our students, we can demonstrate our best efforts to try and experiment with new strategies. Sometimes these strategies will flop, like my attempt at moving seats, but the willingness to honestly recognize an uncomfortable situation and to do *something* is what is most important.

We specifically want to highlight some of our failures in this book as a way to recognize our understanding that everything in teaching is not, in fact, all sunshine and rainbows. But if we aim to be the best versions of ourselves, helping to cultivate the best versions of our students, we have the best chances to do so when we face reality and learn from the great number of difficulties the profession supplies. As Rodgers and Raider-Roth (2006) suggest, these moments of asynchrony can serve as "teachable moments" and "opportunities to develop communication strategies that can help [to regain] connection" (p. 278). Even in these moments where we recognize failures, we can inspire meaningful learning and develop lasting relationships.

If emotional safety is the foundation of effective teaching, which we would argue that it is, then we need to recognize how our conscious and unconscious behaviors and actions create or impede our ability to provide this. Our choices, and the way in which we communicate these choices with students, will help us to either gain or lose their respect and trust, and this ultimately can impact our chances to inspire meaningful learning.

Creating and fostering an emotionally safe classroom environment is probably the most difficult thing to do in teaching. While it can be enticing to focus only on the pedagogical methods that use our capacity to think, create, and analyze the data that result from student work, we are also teaching humans how to be human.

If photosynthesis is the process of learning, then what happens when a plant is exposed to sunlight (the new knowledge)? The size of the pot, the contents of the soil, and the strength of the container for said potted plant are actually very important. And is the plant *watered*? The classroom climate must be *maintained* in much the same way. The teacher is the gardener, and they must stay vigilant. For a person to feel safe in an environment, they will need to see the teacher take both intellectual and emotional risks. They will need to see the teacher do it *first*. And they will need to observe their classmates taking risks, being vulnerable, and being protected by the environment the teacher has built and encouraged.

When we create an emotionally safe space, we, too, will experience that feeling of belonging in a classroom. It is just that it starts with *us*, and we have to have the wherewithal, the capacity, the intention, the presence, and the know-how to do it. If we can create this space, we do it with the knowledge that human connection is the glue that holds it all together. That in relationship, we are complete, whole, and at peace. When we feel at peace, we can be fully present. When we are fully present, we can hear and see others; we look beyond ourselves.

The important thing to remember is that we are human, too. We do this for our students to teach them how to become healthy, flourishing individuals who care about the world outside of themselves. We do it to become whole ourselves, not at the expense of anyone else, but in communion with them, in this learning community of fellow humans that has the power to be entirely transformative. As Laverty (2006) says, "To teach is to intervene in one's own and in another's becoming" (p. 35). This is the essence of this book. We have the capacity to change the lives of others through our teaching, and through our teaching, our lives will be changed. May we all remember just how important our words and our actions really are, especially in the context of a classroom.

Reflective Activities

- Identify a place/person that makes you feel safe. What about that place/person makes you feel safe?

- Recall a time when you or a student may have felt unsafe in your classroom. How did you handle it? After reflecting, would you have handled it in the same way? Why or why not?

- Consider specific ways you explicitly work toward creating emotional safety in your classroom. How do you determine the effectiveness of these strategies? Are there additional methods you could employ to determine their effectiveness?

- Consider the following question, as asked by Rolón-Dow (2005): "How might teachers' views of students and relationships with families be altered if professional development activities involved the community as a center for learning?" (p. 105)

- Think of a lesson you currently teach. What are some questions you could ask to encourage students to build emotional connections with their peers during this lesson?

- Reflect upon your listening in the classroom. What percentage of class time are you speaking during a typical lesson? What percentage of time are you listening?

  _____
  _____

- Create a plan to evaluate the overall feelings of emotional safety in your classroom. Set a short-term goal to help you set this plan in motion.

  _____
  _____
  _____

References

Angelou, M. (1993). *On the pulse of morning*. New York: Random House.

Arao, B., & Clemens, K. (2013). From safe spaces to brave spaces: A new way to frame dialogue around diversity and social justice. In L. Landreman (Ed.), *The art of effective facilitation: Reflections from social justice educators* (pp. 135–150). Sterling, VA: Stylus.

Brown, B. (2013). *Daring greatly: How the courage to be vulnerable transforms the way we live, love, parent and lead*. London: Portfolio Penguin.

Brown, B. (2021). *Atlas of the heart: Mapping meaningful connection and the language of human experience* (1st ed.). New York: Random House.

Garrison, J. (1996). A Deweyan theory of democratic listening. *Educational Theory, 46*, 429–451. https://doi.org/10.1111/j.1741-5446.1996.00429.x

hooks, b. (2000). *All about love: New visions*. New York: William Morrow.

Laverty, M. (2006). Philosophy of education: Overcoming the theory-practice divide. *Paideusis, 15*(1), 31–44.

Nhất Hạnh, T. (2001/2009). *You are here: Discovering the magic of the present moment*. Boulder, CO: Shambhala Publications, Inc.

Noddings, N. (2013). *Caring: A relational approach to ethics and moral education*. Berkeley, CA: University of California Press.

Ricketts, R. (2021). *Do better: Spiritual activism for fighting and healing from white supremacy*. New York: Simon & Schuster.

Rizzolatti, G., & Craighero, L. (2005). Mirror neuron: A neurological approach to empathy. In J. P. Changeux, A. R. Damasio, W. Singer, & Y. Christen (Eds.), *Neurobiology of human values. Research and perspectives in neurosciences*. Berlin, Heidelberg: Springer. https://doi.org/10.1007/3-540-29803-7_9

Rodgers, C. R., & Raider-Roth, M. B. (2006). Presence in teaching. *Teachers and Teaching: Theory and Practice, 12*, 265–287. https://doi.org/10.1080/13450600500467548

Rolón-Dow, C. (2005). Critical care: A color(full) analysis of care narratives in the schooling experiences of Puerto Rican girls. *American Educational Research Journal, 42*, 77–111.

Seider, S., & Graves, D. (2020). *Schooling for critical consciousness: Engaging Black and Latinx youth in analyzing, navigating, and challenging racial injustice*. Cambridge, MA: Harvard Education Press. Virtues Project. https://www.virtuesproject.com/

Wilson, T. D. (2002). *Strangers to ourselves: Discovering the adaptive unconscious*. Cambridge, MA & London, England: The Belknap Press of Harvard University Press.

5

Providing Meaningful Feedback

How Intentional Communication Through Feedback Encourages Student and Educator Growth

Feedback serves as an important form of communication with our students and therefore holds importance in fostering emotional safety and subsequently improving the environment for success in learning. Nhất Hạnh (2001/2009) writes in his book *You Are Here*, that "shining the light of our mindfulness on a situation" is the means for providing feedback to another. He describes how the brothers "shine a light" on a fellow monk and "tell him how they see him" (p. 59). This relates directly to the process of giving feedback because a teacher has a two-fold responsibility: to make the student feel seen and to highlight (or "illuminate") where the student is in their learning process. The role of the teacher is to see, to show, and to guide.

The process of feedback-giving really does hold, at its heart, this principle of illumination. The teacher recognizes the light in the student and, at the same time, shines a light upon this person, so that they can see just where they are and know they are not alone, whatever their academic struggles might be. A teacher must lovingly help a student identify where the student is in their learning journey, as well as demonstrate what comes next, by elucidating the path ahead. It is the job of the teacher to understand and communicate both the current capabilities and future potential of the student. This is one of the most powerful, and difficult, skills of being a teacher.

Kate once called feedback "warm" and "cool" but, after reading Brown's (2013) *Daring Greatly*, where she learned about the "let me sit beside you" idea, she changed her language to match Brown's. Brown describes the typical process as a teacher's sitting across from a student and passing judgment upon them, unaware of the power structure being reinforced. Brown uses the phrase "opportunity for growth" in place of "cool" feedback. Likewise, Kate now uses "strengths" rather than "warm" feedback, because Brown emphasizes that it's not about being "mean" or "nice": it's not the feedback we are trying to qualify but the work. The purpose of the feedback is to give meaningful comments that will allow the person to improve, learn, and grow. Rather than labeling the giving of feedback based upon how it will be received, the attention must be on the product itself. The feedback is not about the one judging, but about the learner's improving the product. As Brown says, "People are desperate for feedback – we all want to grow. We just need to learn how to give feedback in a way that inspires growth and engagement" (p. 198). Rather than shutting someone down, feedback given in this way builds them up. Students receiving feedback from a teacher who believes that their growth is inevitable will be most poised for success. In turn, a student will also learn through this process how to give feedback to peers.

Based upon how we see ourselves and our role in the life of the person whose brain we are responsible for shaping, we may consider giving feedback differently. Some educators may believe that the feedback-giving process is ultimately about their *own* mastery, skills, qualifications, and expertise and how it is reflected in their students' work. These individuals may think, "I see such and such and it's not up to the level I believe makes for something good/beautiful/correct/acceptable/true." If, however, we believe our position of power is as a side-by-side sojourner with our fellow human, a learner like us on a different place on the path (not level) of the journey, we will be linking arms and doing our best to identify both of our places for growth. This dedication to humility will keep us in the "beginner's mind" and will be felt by those with whom we are in the communion of learning.

Giving good feedback is about truly seeing the individual in front of you and the work they have produced. Giving good feedback means approaching the process with open eyes and open heart, free of preconceived notions and already-decided-upon judgment. Giving good feedback is hard to do, because it is tempting to make decisions in advance about a student to speed things up. And expediency is necessary when teaching hundreds of students in many class sections. (We will discuss how to counter such bias in Chapter 9.)

The high number of students in each class and the high number of sections we are required to teach show unequivocally that most educational systems in this country do not truly value feedback. If the school institution truly valued feedback, class size would be much smaller, allowing time for greater student-teacher interaction. Kate received constant and exceptionally thoughtful and detailed feedback from each of her teachers in her small classes in the private Quaker school that she attended from grades 5 to 12.

This gave her the room to grow and the inspiration to improve. Her high school teachers wrote long paragraphs to her every week in all her subjects and then extensive reports at the end of each marking period, because they had the time to do it, teaching, at most, 50 students. They also were able to meet with her in person nearly every day, as well as outside of class during ample study hall periods and after school. In addition, every class day for the entire high school began with a meeting with a small group and an advisor. There were multiple opportunities each day for feedback and affirmation from adults who were able to be deeply invested in a relatively small number of students. Educational settings that can provide these types of meaningful feedback are uncommon, especially in the public school system, but *would* be possible to achieve with systemic changes.

The Importance of Timely Feedback

Time is undoubtedly an important consideration. Without it, valuable feedback is very much impossible. We all know time matters, too, because feedback must be *timely* in order to be most effective. We argue that the benefits of using your time to provide thoughtful and individualized feedback fully justify the time commitment.

In Val's work with student teachers, she is regularly reminded of the importance of timely feedback and has heard a number of student teachers frustrated by observers who have not provided immediate feedback. These student interns would explain that, with all that occurs during a teaching day and week, it was often difficult to remember the details of the lesson and the responses of the students when feedback was provided days or weeks later. Val would continue to remind them to recognize how *their* desire for feedback is similar to that of the students they teach.

Feedback is most meaningful when it is in real time and when one is able to compare their own initial performance reflections to their observable performance. This immediacy in feedback is not only expected by students (Choy, McNickle, & Clayton, 2002) but is also effective in supporting student motivation and in shaping behavior (Anderson, 2004). We have also found timely feedback, particularly the immediate recognition of strengths to have a profoundly positive impact on student-teacher relationships. Students, especially those at the higher level, recognize the effort that timely feedback requires and often express appreciation. Regardless of the level of appreciation though, since many of us will likely not get professions of gratitude, it ultimately is best for student learning and that is reason enough to prioritize providing feedback.

Suggestions for the Feedback Process

We suggest beginning the feedback process by identifying and praising all the strengths and evidence of growth and sharing these first. Next, find opportunities for growth. Finally, wrap up with a couple more strengths. Think of it as a constructive feedback sandwich.

Acknowledging student strengths is the first step, and often one that can be looked over or generalized. Student strengths, like our recognition of areas for growth, should be specific and detailed. Rather than writing "great work," it is much more useful to write something like, "I appreciate how you connected [topic] to [topic] here. It shows that you have a deep understanding of the issue." Any time we can thoughtfully and intentionally recognize highly specific decisions made and actions taken by another, we will strengthen the habit loop.

Next, we look for opportunities for growth. The communication of these opportunities should be accompanied by examples and/or specific strategies for the student to improve in this area. Without this step, it will likely be difficult for most students to course-correct on their own. For example, if we tell a student to "include more of your evaluation," we can provide them with examples of evaluative words (e.g. beneficial, convincing, damaging) or rewrite one of their sentences in a way that includes this language. We can also point them to specific resources and/or previous assignments or lessons to further develop their learning.

Here it is important to consider the number of opportunities for growth provided in the feedback. We believe that there should be balance in the number of strengths and growth opportunities recognized and that each piece of student work should receive both. Those with outstanding work should recognize that there are always areas to improve in addition to their existing strengths. Those who have many areas to improve also should know multiple areas in which they have demonstrated mastery, growth, and/or progress.

It is also important to give honest and authentic feedback, rooted in what you find in the work *and* in the context of who the student is, *not* shadowed by your expectations of them. Instead, in the context of what you know about them – a diagnosis, a learning difference, a divorce, a loss, a tendency – hold that person as precious and fragile, approaching them tenderly and gently. Look at the outcome not as a finished product – the student is not finished growing and becoming and neither are you – but as a Polaroid snapshot, an *in-medias-res* moment. We are witnesses to who that person was being at that moment and what that person was shining forth then. How we respond to this human in this time will shape their future moments, their future learning, and potentially their future achievement.

This approach to teaching is a moment-in-time process – a "who-one-is-at-this-moment" instant of reality, and by the time we, the teacher, are reading this work, the author of what we are reading has already changed. The neural traces in their brain are growing at a rapid-fire pace and the learning is so quick and so malleable, we are already archeologists if we wait a week to give feedback.

A student shines forth what their understanding is in that moment and then we "feed" it "back." It must be an "I see" and then a whole lot of curiosity. "What do you mean by this?" and "Tell me more about that," and "I think I see what you are saying and I believe I can guess where you are headed… where are you taking this next?"

The aim is growth – learning and growth. The feedback has to be as frequent as sunlight and water, not fertilizer. Fertilizer is a couple of times a year. Sunshine needs to be pretty constant. And so the feedback is really a shining forth of the light, the illumination of thinking, and the spotlighting of connections made. Feedback is a lighting up and a highlighting of the aspects of the work a teacher can see and identify as evidence of thinking that happened and what's coming next.

We need to remind students of these truths when we present them with our feedback, which is another crucial step in the feedback process. If students are not *prepared* to receive constructive feedback, our time and effort in providing feedback will be wasted. It becomes important to explicitly remind students, maybe even *each* time feedback is provided, of its importance for growth. Brené Brown has created an "Engaged Feedback Checklist" in which she outlines statements that demonstrate readiness to give feedback. This checklist could be adapted for students or you could create your own "Readiness for Receiving Feedback" checklist. Ours would include the following statements:

- ◆ I understand that the goal of the feedback is to help me become a better version of myself
- ◆ I am open and ready to accept how another person interprets my work/writing
- ◆ I recognize that I may be surprised by some feedback as we all have blind spots that we do not recognize until they are pointed out to us
- ◆ I am ready to ask questions if I do not fully understand the feedback provided
- ◆ I am ready to grow and learn

Suggestions for Informal Feedback

Recognizing areas for growth also applies when we consider whether and how to correct students outside of formal assessments. Most of us experience moments of student error throughout a lesson, whether related to grammar or content.

Our general guides for deciding when to correct a student:

- Is it related to the communicated learning task? (Do they expect the feedback?)
- Was my feedback solicited? (Do they want the feedback?)
- Is it necessary now? (Do they need the feedback?)

If Val has not communicated that she will be assessing students on a task, like the formality of their speech during a class discussion or their spelling in a reflection assignment, she will not provide feedback on that particular item. These communications can be part of the classroom expectations set at the beginning of the year, a rubric for an assignment, or a simple "I will be looking for you to..." before a task begins. She knows how it feels to receive unsolicited "advice" as an adult for something unrelated to a conversation and would not want students to have that feeling in her classroom. When correcting, she needs to determine whether student confidence, risk-taking, and creativity of her students are more important than the correction of the error, as these may be in jeopardy if she chooses to correct the student.

An exception to this rule is offensive speech, including unintentionally offensive speech, as these are corrections necessary for the safety of all students and also for the future knowledge and success of the offending individual. Importantly, the students in her classroom know how she plans to address offensive speech if it arises and how she expects them to address it themselves, and these are discussed as part of her classroom expectations.

Another exception would be if the error could significantly affect the learning of that particular student or another. In these cases, and especially if the error was presented to a student audience, she would reword the student's contribution with the correction and follow up with the student later, if necessary. On occasion, she has also thanked students for allowing for the opportunity for class growth by bringing to our attention a common misconception.

Val recognizes that her choices in choosing to address student error are related to her subject and further recognizes that teachers of different subjects (e.g. languages) may find the choice to correct students during informal times to be more pressing.

When Kate presents feedback, she considers the approach from a relational standpoint. She decides if there is enough trust built between them that she can point out something that needs to be changed. Then she will usually ask whether the person would like help or correcting. She might say something like, "Would you like my feedback?" or, "Can I make a suggestion?" These require asking permission from the person, thereby giving them choice and not forcing her will upon them. This preserves trust and builds mutual respect.

We have also observed the impacts of nonverbal feedback in the classroom. We should notice and reflect upon both the direction and frequency of our gaze, our physical nearness to students throughout a lesson, our pauses in speech, and our facial expressions. These actions serve as methods of informal feedback and students will adjust their behaviors in response to them. We all know how we respond when we are on our phones during a meeting and the presenter walks nearer to us or how we know to speak louder when someone leans toward us when listening. These actions are interpreted, rightfully, as feedback and should be reflected upon and considered carefully in the classroom.

The Lasting Impacts of Feedback

Each of us, as we are sure many of you can relate, has memories of receiving feedback from teachers that impacted us in both positive and negative ways.

KMH: During my freshman year of college, after writing a paper on Kafka, my TA told me I just wasn't that good at writing. I asked him what I could do to improve my writing and he said, "Not much. You're just not that good a writer."

So I ditched my dream of majoring in English literature and chose to pursue Ecology and

Evolutionary Biology, instead. The beauty of this newish 4 billion-year-old planet in the scheme of the 14 billion-year-old universe appealed to me. And my Biology TA from Vancouver gave me excellent feedback on my weekly lab reports. He helped me improve and it felt amazing. Also, we got to pith a live frog and experiment with its heart by shooting caffeine into it. Poor frog. Lucky me.

Truly, I am amazed every day by the beauty of my incredible students, and I simply want to continue to strive to get the giving of feedback right. Learning to give feedback as an educator is an ongoing process of growth. Learning to take feedback is even harder.

We receive critique throughout our school years but rarely learn to give effective feedback ourselves. And even though we receive feedback, we don't ever really learn to receive feedback fruitfully. Both skills must be taught, to be used in all relationships of our lives.

VK: The first memory I have of teacher feedback was from my seventh-grade year. My teacher was walking around the room, handing back work to the class. She stopped when she returned my assignment to tell me that the way I dotted each letter *i* was childish. My twelve-year-old self believed I was being creative by dotting them with little circles and occasionally dotting the *i* in Valerie with a smiley face. From then on, each time I did not dot the *i* "properly," a red pen crossed out the offending tittle. (Yes, that is the actual word for the superscript dot.) While I did ultimately have a good relationship with that teacher and this anecdote may seem silly, her criticism was a big-time joy-killer, and it stood out as one of my only three memories of receiving feedback in my pre-college schooling years.

The second, another joy-killer, was feedback on a family history project in which I had become fully invested. My paternal grandmother kept meticulous records of our family history, including accounts of our ancestors coming to the United States. She even made a folder for each of her 20+ grandchildren with the details of our family tree and photos. Part of the project was to make diary entries from a chosen ancestor and, since I happened to have a lot of information on this thanks to my thoughtful Nanny as well as the motivation to complete additional research, I was able to include much more detail than the teacher apparently expected. When the project was returned, I realized that she had taken off an entire letter grade because she determined that my level of detail was "suspicious." Rather than commending my choice to go all-in on a project of personal importance for me, she accused me of cheating. I was so angry that I didn't even bother to address it with her and accepted the lower grade. Probably unsurprisingly, I also put less effort into the class for the remainder of the year.

The last piece of feedback, the only positive one I can recall, was conveyed to the entire class, so the feelings of embarrassment mixed with pride likely accounted for the vivid memory. Upon Kate's insistence, I will share this memory, too. The teacher of my law class in high school had tasked the students with selecting the most appropriate panel of jurists from a large jury "pool" for a hypothetical case. He had pre-selected the jurists that would have been most partial to the defense's case. Along with one other student in his teaching career, I had been able to decipher the exact jurists that he had preselected.

As Kate and Val discussed afterward, Val's memories of each of these experiences of receiving feedback provoked intense emotion, resulting in her ability to recall each – the belittling regarding the tittle, the disrespect of the knowledge and connection to her family in her research, and the pride and validation in a skill she believed that she might have, respectively. We must remember how intensely a student can feel, particularly during their most formative teenage years, when we give feedback. To remind the reader, Kate changed her career path as a result of one instructor's careless feedback. Here, empathy can be the single most important brain skill to yield when considering feedback-giving.

Feedback also has a powerful impact on our relationships with students, which we may not consciously notice at times. Spending the time to really examine a student's work is a way to show that you are listening and that you value the student's growth. Giving feedback is an important way to show that you care about *each* student, even those who are not as vocal in the classroom. Conversely, providing flippant or general feedback likely will result in students not taking the assessment or activity seriously or damaging the student-teacher relationship.

Val distinctly remembers a friend copying others' assignments in high school, eventually even photocopying all packet pages after page one, despite the fact that she found the content interesting, because the teacher "never read [the completed assignments] anyway." She felt that way because of the general "good!" and "nice work!" comments written on the assignments. It seemed that no care was taken by the teacher to ensure that student thought was put into the assignment, so her friend didn't put any thought into it either. Unsurprisingly, the students did not have a good relationship with this teacher, although she was pleasant and the topics of the class were compelling.

The Role of Grades in the Feedback-Giving Process

So, if we place so much importance on the feedback, then what becomes the importance of grading, actually assigning a letter or number to a student's work?

The act of grading, for us, produces skepticism regarding its usefulness. We believe it is one of our deepest sources of social reproduction because it's the nexus of where a teacher's background, level of understanding, adaptive unconscious, and implicit biases all come together in a sort of "intersectionality of judgment," so to speak. Each person doing any sort of assessment of another automatically places value judgments upon the other based upon a whole slew of factors. As two educators who try to actively consider how oppression is perpetuated in the classroom, this is an area of high interest for us. While we recognize that the mandatory and obsessive sorting and reporting on student "progress" is a tradition of the American education system that is unlikely to change overnight, we also recognize that the real learning happens in the feedback, *not* in the rating, sorting, and ranking.

Who decides what is good? Who decides what's good enough? What is correct? Who is right? How much of a role do our biases play when grading? Is anonymous grading a solution or even a realistic option? Can we effectively combat biases in a way that can render grading accurate?

This is why we place so much importance on the feedback as opposed to merely the grade. The feedback provides the opportunity to decide for another human who they are and what they can become, based upon a few visible pieces of evidence in the context of *many* invisible and unknown data. Often in a vacuum, as we are tired and overworked, we help build the bricks of the walls that will limit and funnel a human into the choices of their future. These grades we (often) (arbitrarily) decide upon for humans become the walls, the limitations for our students.

While we see the potential drawbacks of grading, we also concede that evaluating student work can be useful as a way to determine our effectiveness as teachers. That is to say, the grades matter more for determining our *own* effectiveness, rather than the extent of the student's actual learning. Instead of serving as a way to catch a student in their confusion, determining that this confusion is the end of their learning on the topic, it should be a check of our effectiveness and a tool for future learning. This applies to both our methods and our instruments of assessment. Grading should help us to determine any areas of confusion or ineffectiveness and think about how we, as educators, can adapt our teaching to benefit our students' learning.

The Role of Feedback in Creating Lasting Beliefs About the Self

The human brain believes what it hears and, in the context of a student listening to a teacher, students generally default to accepting a teacher's beliefs about them as true. If a teacher tells a student they cannot write, or they cannot do something well, that message sinks in as truth. The student then thinks that thought and it becomes a well-worn neural pathway, forming a way of thinking about themselves that is self-limiting. (Why do so many people believe they are "bad" at math?) The teacher makes an arbitrary choice based on their mood or their subjective perceptions, and this "ruling" which is little more than a random musing, one could argue, has the power to become a lasting belief. As Kwik (2023) writes in *Limitless*:

> Often when you put a label on someone or something, you create a limit. The label becomes the limitation. Adults have to be very careful with their external words because these quickly become a child's internal words.
>
> (p. 6)

The feedback we give to students becomes their beliefs about themselves. And, although we often don't have the brain power on a daily basis to recognize this truth, we are brain-shapers.

Up until this point we have discussed the importance of teacher-to-student feedback but, of course, there are so many other ways in which feedback enters the classroom. We will briefly discuss some of these types of feedback here – student-to-student feedback, administrator-to-teacher feedback, and student-to-teacher feedback – and then discuss colleague-to-colleague feedback in greater depth in Chapter 8.

Student-to-Student Feedback

Constructive peer feedback, while useful in terms of community-building and helping students to consider alternate ways of thinking, can be especially difficult for students to give and receive. As educators, we serve an important role in assisting students in their ability to provide and accept such feedback.

Each of us has experimented with ways to allow students to most effectively provide feedback to one another. For Val, successful strategies have included asking students to write down their observations about another's strengths (2) and an area for growth (1) and then modeling her own feedback aloud, providing sentence starters or a list of feedback options for students to choose from. Alternatively, she has asked students to provide only positive feedback to one another as areas for growth tend to be the more difficult of the two. In terms of constructive feedback on writing, Val has also found success using groups of three and a conversational feedback protocol to aid students in identifying areas to improve. Prompts for this may include the following:

- ◆ Identify specific sentences in which the argument is well-supported. Discuss what makes this evidence strong.

- Identify one area of confusion in the writing or one area in which the evidence could be strengthened. Discuss how this section is interpreted by the reader and make at least one suggestion to strengthen the writing.

In Kate's classroom, she uses multiple methods for student-to-student feedback. At times, she asks students to complete a Google Form to grade peers based on rubrics either created by Kate, her teaching team, or the students themselves. She also asks the students to complete an open-ended "glow, grow, glow" feedback sandwich. Other times, she holds meetings with student groups to determine a consensus on the grading rubric before selecting the final grade for group presentations, in which Kate retains the final say. Additionally, she discusses assessment preparation with students and guides students to assess the preparation of their peers based on the following questions:

- Where do you differ in your learning experiences and learning outcomes? Where do you coincide?
- Where do you differ in your goals? Where do you coincide?
- What discoveries have you made about yourself during the conversation?
- What discoveries have you made about your partner during the conversation?
- What wonderings do you have based on this discussion?

There are many ways to approach peer feedback but we have found that developing a protocol routine is most effective. A colleague utilizes the "rose, thorn, bud" peer assessment approach in which students recognize a strength, an area for growth, and an emerging idea. Kate has spent many hours discussing the implementation of peer feedback with this colleague in their respective science classrooms. Together, they realized the power of peer feedback as a formative and brain-changing experience for their students that also serves as a path for teaching empathy. They have found that peer feedback is most profound when it causes students to think about, and share, how they learn and the process that allows them to learn best. She intentionally designs feedback processes, protocols, and questions with this in mind. Students are then able to see alternative methods for learning, some of which may fit better with their learning style than the methods proposed by the teacher.

Administrator-to-Teacher Feedback

In setting up students to receive feedback, whether our own or from their peers, it is useful to remind ourselves of the feelings that accompany its reception. Even if we are far removed from being in the classroom ourselves, we all are likely familiar with the feeling of judgment through our administrator observations. When we consider what feels the most and least comfortable during the observation process, we can recognize that it is no different than the feedback and grading process for students. We hope that administrators provide us affirmation during the observation and timely feedback afterward, recognize our strengths as well as the most important areas to grow, use details to support their observations (e.g. "There was 5 minutes allotted for discussion" vs. "The discussion was too short"), and make relevant suggestions that can help us to move forward. Getting the final rubric, essentially our grade, can be uncomfortable, but if we have had a meaningful discussion about the observation first, then this becomes less painful.

While this observation process, in theory, can be completed by any administrator, we have found that the most useful observations to advance our teaching were completed by those who had specific subject knowledge, were aware of our goals in the classroom, and could provide specific examples to accompany their suggestions. Unfortunately, for many school districts, this is not the case, and, as a result, the feedback process for teachers is not as valuable as it could be otherwise.

A research study by Cherasaro, Brodersen, Reale, and Yanoski (2016) examined how teachers value and use evaluative feedback in order to support efforts to increase teacher effectiveness. They made the following suggestions for educational leaders based on their findings:

- Reviewing evaluator training and guidance on feedback to teachers to identify ways to strengthen the usefulness of the feedback.
- Examining policies related to the usefulness of feedback or collecting data to identify potential barriers to providing useful feedback.
- Considering ways to ensure that feedback is frequent, is timely, and includes specific suggestions to improve content and subject knowledge, instructional strategies, classroom management strategies, and recommendations for finding resources or professional development opportunities.
- Targeting suggestions to improve content and subject knowledge and classroom management because more than half of teachers indicated that these suggestions were important for responding to

feedback, but less than half said that these suggestions were provided in the feedback they received.
- Focusing on ways to build evaluator credibility because perceptions of evaluator credibility were strongly correlated with teachers' perceptions of the usefulness of the feedback.
- Where teachers have less favorable ratings of evaluator credibility, considering ways to build evaluators' knowledge of the content or subject being evaluated, knowledge of how students learn, knowledge of teaching practices, understanding of the curriculum being observed, and understanding of the established teacher evaluation system.

(p. 11)

Rather than traditional administrator observations, we found success in an alternative evaluation model, aptly called the Alternative Evaluation model in the district in which we work/worked. We highly recommend this collaborative process as an option for districts and administrators who want teachers to take specific action to solve problems that they have encountered in the classroom. In this model, teachers selected problems of practice in their own teaching to address, either alone or with a peer, and an administrator served as an observer and feedback-provider of this project. These self-selected projects allowed each of us and our respective partners to receive targeted feedback and suggestions that made meaningful impacts on our effectiveness as teachers. We will discuss these projects in more depth in Chapter 8 as they enabled us to receive effective peer feedback from colleagues.

Student-to-Teacher Feedback

The most important feedback we can receive, however, and the feedback that should hold the most weight, is from the students themselves. We need to know from them whether we are meeting their needs. Even if we may not agree with the feedback they provide (and we should do some reflection to determine why this is), the act of collecting student feedback demonstrates that we value their thoughts and suggestions.

Allowing students to provide feedback on our teaching is necessary for our growth, to develop the best lessons and assessments for our students, and also to identify personal areas in which we need to grow. The we-are-in-this-together mentality that we hope to cultivate means that the feedback process is not shaped by ego and power but rather by humility and service. When we provide these opportunities to students, we show that we respect and value their thoughts and model how we want them to receive our feedback. Receiving student feedback, on top of our already demanding emotional workload, can be exhausting or hurtful to students of any age and may make some teachers avoid it as much as possible. Regardless, we need to do this often for our students and for ourselves.

VK: As a new teacher, I remember feeling a sense of dread when collecting formal feedback on my teaching. I knew it was important, so while most feedback was informal (ex. asking students about a lesson immediately afterward), I continued to collect formal feedback a minimum of twice a year. I also developed some strategies to make me feel less like vomiting before reading them:

- I stated my intentions beforehand, verbally and written on the form, and reminded students how much I valued their honest feedback. I found that this helped students to take it more seriously and actually write more.
- I always began by asking about what *was* working well.
- I included questions about student responsibility as well as teacher responsibility ex. "How can the teacher help you…?" and "Is there anything that you can do…?"
- I chose to read them during times of low teacher stress (ex. Friday afternoons, Saturday mornings, after completing all my grading).
- I gave myself rewards – generally delicious food.
- I talked out the difficult feedback with colleagues that I trusted and who knew me and my teaching.
- I reminded myself that this is how we expect the students to grow and that I was just putting myself in their shoes.

Before I left teaching high school, I formally collected student feedback, written or video, each marking period and after project-based assessments and was able to become a more responsive teacher as a result. I also felt, and so did the students based on their feedback, that I grew closer to them. The students always recognized and appreciated when changes were made based on their feedback, and I could see higher engagement levels from those students, particularly those who typically had low engagement levels in class.

As I write this, I hear the "ding" of my email. The results from the instructional surveys from my last semester teaching pre-service teachers are released. I feel the familiar heaviness in my chest and feel my heart pumping more quickly than it had been moments ago. I find myself instinctively thinking about what I have to do for the rest of the morning and whether I should put off reading the results until a period of free time after which I can complete a relaxing activity (gardening is my go-to these days). Instead, since I have a relatively stress-free morning, which is why I had time to write in the first place, I take a deep breath and click on the link.

Having just read them, I am breathing normally again and laughing at myself for being nervous beforehand. No matter how well I think I know the students and can anticipate their feedback, I guess there is always a fear that there will be some surprise indicating that I had misinterpreted a student's needs. There is always a (now conscious) fear that I have been unable to fulfill student needs while simultaneously creating an environment of discomfort that prevented them from telling me during the semester. I recognize that no matter what, I would appreciate the opportunity for growth, but I also recognize that feelings happen. In this case, luckily, I fully understand and anticipate the feedback provided. I greatly appreciate the students who took the time to write thoughtful and specific feedback and recognized (and valued) the feedback process that I was aiming to model for them. The students highlighted their appreciation of my feedback-giving because they found it "useful, practical, and affirming," "delivered with grace," "compassionate," "positive… as well as [acknowledging] areas to improve upon," and "kind but effective."

The choice of the word "but" in "kind but effective" stood out to both Kate and Val, as we discussed this feedback, and we agreed it spoke volumes. Why can't feedback be both kind *and* effective? Shouldn't this be the expectation? Unfortunately, the expectation is that an observer is *either* kind *or* provides constructive feedback, not both. This should not be the case. We each do our best to provide fair feedback that does not shy away from confronting areas for growth – we aim to be both kind *and* effective.

We must be ever mindful of the power of language. If we are able to show students that we care about them, through our words and actions, then feedback *to* and *from* them can be more readily accepted, and therefore be "effective." We also find it very useful to be reminded of the feelings that accompany the anticipation of judgment. These are feelings that our students may experience often, some with each assessment received, and relating to this experience serves as an important reminder of what we hope for when we (all) receive feedback.

When we are able to have students provide unsolicited feedback, although it may not always be what we want to hear, we know that we have created a space in which students feel that their feedback is truly valued and important. These are meaningful moments of relationship-building and community-building.

KMH: Before the winter break I asked students to complete a reflection on the cardiovascular system unit as well as their year in general. I asked them to set goals for themselves for the coming year and to state one thing they had learned from me that would stay with them. This student hadn't completed this task on time and, instead, held on to this memory for all of the break. Then he finally completed it upon our return from winter break and I read it while he was still in the class. He wrote that he was saying it with the "utmost respect" and that he really needed to get it off his chest. I found that to be amazing, first, because it meant that our STR was indeed strong and he felt safe to write it. Also, he cared so much about the goings on in the class that it was bothering him greatly *not* to tell me. He said, in sum, that when I am nice I make the class "awesome," and then sometimes my mood changes abruptly (he said, "at the drop of a hat") and then "the entire classroom feels it." This struck the qualitative researcher in me, and I immediately tuned into the way he used language to explain precisely how he (and how he perceives the class) to feel my mood. I don't know that every student is as tuned in as he is, but it doesn't matter. This was a piercing truth for him, and I was thrilled to know it.

The student went on to explain that I had singled out another student and was asking him to do something about his constant lateness. Apparently, the student said, "Come on, it's Christmas!" and then the author of the feedback said he felt I hadn't taken it as a joke. This was true. I hadn't taken it as a joke, and instead went on a "rant," and "pretty much killed the mood." The best part of this was that in the student's explaining the entire scenario, he goes on to give me the best advice: "take what your students say with a grain of salt." He said, "We are still young adults…I don't know, maybe we don't think like a scientist yet."

So perceptive. So wise. I felt happiness at his openness and joy that he had had the courage to call his teacher out in this way. It provided evidence that I still have a long way to go on working on *always* being kind, gentle, calm, and responsive. In this situation I felt the absence of ego, the presence of peace, and the deep hope in many tomorrows that will allow me to work toward being a more ideal human and ideal teacher. I wrote back to this student who called me out on killing the mood with my lack of humor and my reactive rant:

"Awesome feedback and definitely spot on. My son, Nate, would completely agree with you. As my intention for this year, I am working on being gentler and that means (hopefully) fewer rants and 'taking things with more grace.'"

Here, Kate's response to her student's feedback demonstrated her ability to change her brain. Responding in an appreciative manner also demonstrated her valuing of student perspective and the ability to take feedback with grace. In another recent example, Kate was reminded of the importance of acting upon student feedback to maintain the open and trusting classroom climate that she and her students have worked to build. A student, after quietly collecting data from his peers, asked at the beginning of the period if the class could have more time for their presentations rather than presenting that day, as had been planned. She told him that they would talk about it, and then she overheard him telling his tablemates that he had "tried." Hearing this, she decided to see where the rest of the class stood and asked them to vote with their eyes closed – who was afraid, who was not ready, who needed more time. It was clear that most needed more time. After getting his permission, she shared with the class what she had overheard and that, realizing he was speaking on behalf of his peers, she wanted to give them what they needed – more time. By doing this, she explained she aimed to model understanding and gentleness for them. The group that was ready was able to present that day, and the rest were given the time that they felt they needed to prepare. This choice to honor student feedback was intentional and served to preserve the supportive classroom climate that they had been working to build.

Demonstrating the importance of our students' perspectives, solicited or unsolicited, is one important way we can allow them to gain feelings of empowerment in the classroom. This valuing of and utilizing student feedback serves as a requisite to powerful relationship-building and the foundation of feelings of community.

In our busy educator lives, we may neglect to reflect on the importance of our feedback for our students. However, our communication through feedback contributes significantly to all of the relationships within the classroom as well as the overall classroom dynamic. Eliciting and utilizing student feedback further serves to build student confidence in the teacher and in their own agency. In the next chapter, we will discuss self-awareness and self-regulation to help with the processing of feedback, particularly when it may reveal unwanted behaviors in ourselves.

Reflective Activities

- Discuss with a colleague:
  - How often do you collect feedback on your teaching? Why?

  - What is the best feedback you have received from a student, administrator, or peer? Why? How did this impact your teaching?

  - What was the most difficult feedback you have received? Why? How did this impact your teaching?

  - Do you prefer feedback from administration, peers, or students? Why?

- Consider the feedback experiences you carry from your own education.
  - How did these experiences impact your life? Are you able to identify any beliefs about yourself and your capabilities based upon memorable feedback?

  - Have they impacted how you receive and give feedback?

- Solicit feedback from students about your feedback to find out areas of strength and areas for growth. Does anything surprise you?
  _____
  _____
  _____

- Consider the following questions regarding your comfort levels when receiving feedback.
  - What feelings do you experience when you prepare to hear feedback? Do you consciously prepare to receive feedback?
    _____
    _____
    _____

  - How do you think these feelings are similar or different to your students when encountering feedback?
    _____
    _____
    _____

References

Anderson, T. (2004). Teaching in an online learning context. In T. Anderson & F. Elloumi (Eds.), *Theory and practice of online learning* (pp. 273–294). Athabasca, Alberta, Canada: Athabasca University.

Brown, B. (2013). *Daring greatly: How the courage to be vulnerable transforms the way we live, love, parent and lead.* London: Portfolio Penguin.

Brown, B. (2024). *Engaged feedback checklist.* https://brenebrown.com/resources/the-engaged-feedback-checklist/

Cherasaro, T. L., Brodersen, R. M., Reale, M. L., & Yanoski, D. C. (2016). *Teachers' responses to feedback from evaluators: What feedback characteristics matter? (REL 2017–190).* Washington, DC: U.S. Department of Education, Institute of Education Sciences, National Center for Education Evaluation and Regional Assistance, Regional Educational Laboratory Central.

Choy, S., McNickle, C., & Clayton, B. (2002). *Learner expectations and experiences: An examination of student views of support in online learning.* Kensington Park, SA, Australia: Australian National Training Authority.

Kwik, J. (2023). *Limitless: Upgrade your brain, learn anything faster, and unlock your exceptional life.* Expanded edition. Carlsbad, CA: Hay House.

Nhất Hạnh, T. (2001/2009). *You are here: Discovering the magic of the present moment.* Boulder, CO: Shambhala Publications.

PART II
Looking Inward, Shining Out

6

Increasing Our Self-Awareness

How Self-Reflection and Present-Moment Awareness Transform Teaching and Learning

Up until this point, we have examined aspects of building stronger relationships in the field of education. Much of the remainder of the book will focus more explicitly on learning and being more intentional which can, in turn, benefit our students. If we are not aware of our own emotions and stressors, we cannot be fully present for our students or in the best position to build meaningful relationships. We can also, through modeling and purposeful activities, help them to build these skills for themselves. We need to be committed to identifying aspects of ourselves and our own personal growth, just as we intend to teach our students to do the very same.

hooks (1994), in her essay "Engaged Pedagogy," remarks that "teachers must be actively committed to a process of self-actualization that promotes their own well-being if they are to teach in a manner that empowers students" (p. 14). Indeed, we need to teach with our full authentic selves, as exhausting as that may be, in order to maximize the potential for learning in our classrooms. It is this commitment to bettering ourselves that helps us process and utilize constructive feedback from others, thereby enabling us to accept the truths that shape us for the better. Being able to model this process of self-reflection toward personal growth for our students is one of the best lessons we can provide them to demonstrate the pathway to becoming the best version of oneself.

Present-Moment Awareness

As much as possible, we need to focus on the present in each moment we spend with our students. Nhất Hạnh (2001/2009) reminds us that "the future is being made out of the present, so the best way to take care of the future is to take care of the present moment" (p. 51). Learning to live in the present, without dwelling too much on the past or spending too much time imagining a not-yet-here future, is the surest way to enter into a place of greater self-awareness. In turn, self-awareness enables us to learn self-regulation.

As an educator, or as any person presenting to a group of people, there are a lot of things for our brains to manage. We are constantly multitasking, thinking ahead to later meetings or lessons or emails we need to write, while attempting to monitor each human in the room. We understand the difficulty in being fully present but we also understand the necessity. As we can tell if another person is distracted when we are spending time with them, students can tell when our minds are elsewhere, and this, when no explanation is provided, results in distance. Being fully present for anyone is a gift that allows them to feel worthy of your attention and valued. Individuals in a classroom community need to feel this value in order to want to participate fully, to be fully present themselves. Kate often acknowledges to her students, "There is no place else I would rather be than right here with you," to ensure that they know just how much she values each and every one of them.

The power is in the combination of present-moment awareness and self-awareness, because they are inextricably tied. We want to be fully present so our brains are at optimal functioning, and we want to be able to be the witness of our thoughts. For example, as Kate is speaking to Val right now while she writes, she is aware that Val might think she is rambling, but she chooses to set that aside to be in the present. The self-judgment needs to be put on hold. We need to think about what is most important at that moment. The combination of cultivating and maintaining these habits of mind requires constant vigilance and this is where the cognitive energy must go. We recognize that this is pretty impossible to do all the time. No human can put all of their fears, worries, and concerns entirely on hold, but if we throw ourselves into teaching in the way a brain surgeon throws herself into her work, we can be most effective.

So what is actually happening in the present moment in our brains? We are building our neural traces, as our ribosomes are making the proteins that will connect neurons to one another in new ways. In other words, while it does take time for the process of learning to become ingrained in physical cells in our bodies and brains, the initial awareness of the input data is necessary to allow for that process to occur. We build our brains in real time, in the here and now. We are brain-changers and, in order to be the best type of brain-changer, we must continually change our own brains, too.

Present-moment awareness is the single most powerful agent for changing our brains. Naturally, we are not thinking of the present. Instead, because of the evolution of the human brain, we are danger watchers. Practicing watching one's thoughts is an ability that we can cultivate to allow us to handle the thousand things happening at any given moment in a classroom. Full present-moment awareness, as elusive as it may seem, enables us to see things for what they really are, and not what we wish for them to be. This can help an educator to better serve the exact students in her care.

As Tolle (1999/2004) reminds us:

> Give attention to the present. Give attention to your behavior, to your reactions, moods, thoughts, emotions, fears and desires as they occur in the present. If you can be present enough to watch all those things, not critically or analytically, but nonjudgmentally, then you are dealing with the past and dissolving it through the power of your presence.
>
> (p. 91)

For Kate, the daily habit of journaling serves as a way to learn from interpersonal interactions and the thoughts and emotions that arise from them. This record becomes a source of data that she can revisit. She journals specific experiences that she wants to remember so she can revisit them with a fresh brain and a new perspective. In the absence of the flood of stress hormones that often accompanies a rough day of teaching, a calm mind sheds new light. She also has a daily practice of writing gratitudes. Years of research have shown that acknowledging specific gratitudes improves levels of happiness and overall health (Jans-Beken et al., 2019).

Journaling – and the self-reflection it allows – is a way to prepare our brains for the fresh approach this profession requires daily. Keeping a personal record of one's thoughts and important ideas that come into our worlds – it can be as simple as notes in our phones or an email to ourselves – can be the vehicle for self-reflection.

Increasing Awareness of Our Emotions

Awareness of one's own conscious and unconscious emotions and physical reactions is paramount to living an authentic life. While a person may consciously believe that they are engaging in positive social interactions or are comfortable with individuals of different identity groups, their unconscious behaviors may suggest otherwise and sabotage these relationships.

Fortunately, many researchers have designed strategies to help individuals connect with and process their emotions and automatic reactions. Some reading suggestions on this topic include

- *Blindspot: Hidden Biases of Good People* by Anthony Greenwald and Mahzarin Banaji
- *My Grandmother's Hands: Racialized Trauma and the Pathway to Mending Our Hearts and Bodies* by Resmaa Menakem
- *The Body Keeps the Score: Brain, Mind, and Body in the Healing of Trauma* by Bessel A. van der Kolk
- *The Power of Now: A Guide to Spiritual Enlightenment* by Eckhart Tolle
- *Emotions Revealed: Recognizing Faces and Feelings to Improve Communication and Emotional Life* by Paul Ekman

Ekman (2007) explains,

We don't choose how we look and sound or what we are impelled to do and say when we are emotional any more than we choose when to become emotional. But we can learn to moderate emotional behavior we would regret afterward, to inhibit or subdue our expressions, to prevent or temper our actions or words.

(p. 53)

To do this, we need to pay attention to how our bodies react to stimuli. While we may not be able to immediately pinpoint our exact emotions, this recognition of our own physical responses can bring us more awareness of our emotional state. This bringing the unconscious to light allows us a greater opportunity to decide how to respond. These responses can be instrumental in strengthening or straining relationships, the importance of which we have discussed in previous chapters. With practice, we can even learn to make certain responses automatic, as those of us who drive have learned to brake and turn the wheel automatically in the face of danger while driving (Ekman, 2007).

While the world around us cannot stop, we can stop ourselves in the moment to take a break when we sense our emotions coming too strongly. Sometimes we just need to press the pause button. Pausing allows us the opportunity to recalibrate and determine whether our emotional response is appropriate or inappropriate for the situation. It can also provide us the moment needed to consider the weight of our words and the impact they may have on another's emotions.

Strategies for Increasing Awareness of Others' Emotions

Awareness of the emotions of others is also key as it is beneficial both for classroom management as well as relationship-building. Reading faces, body language, and behavior, while usually difficult tasks, can provide invaluable insight into another's emotional state and can help us to alter our reactions. Whether it is recognizing facial changes – which research suggests are universal, although rules about the management and display of these emotions may differ from culture to culture (Ekman, 2007) – or noticing a student's tendency to ask to go to the bathroom when tasked with independent work, our recognition of the stimuli leading to the response is the key to successful learning. Of course, reading every student throughout each class period is an exceptionally difficult task, which is another one of the many reasons that we would argue that smaller class sizes are necessary.

Assisting students with exploring awareness of emotions can have similar benefits. We can help students to practice identifying their own conscious and unconscious reactions in response to content material. Examples of questions can include

- How does that make you feel?
- Do you notice any physical changes in your body as you watch/learn about this topic?
- What might these responses suggest about how you feel?

Activities that prompt students to "read" others – maybe characters in a book or film or individuals depicted in primary sources – can be useful for helping to identify and respond to the emotions of others and can be especially important for individuals who have difficulty reading social cues. Not only can such activities help students to build social skills, but it can also help them to recognize how they process their own emotions.

Cultivating a Growth Mindset

Kate often discusses the importance of embracing a growth mindset, with students and other educators. She explains how a "fixed" mindset results in the belief that intelligence is static, making a person avoid challenges, give up, see effort as pointless, or see the success of others as a threat (Dweck, 2007). A "growth" mindset, on the other hand, allows for the belief that intelligence is variable, leading to the willingness to learn and improve. This mindset encourages embracing challenges, persisting in the face of setbacks, appreciating effort as a means to mastery, and learning from the success of others. Not only is intelligence variable, but it can actually be enhanced through practice and lots of fruitful failure.

As educators, and humans who want to be better people tomorrow than we were yesterday, we should strive for a growth mindset and the "I don't know that *yet*" attitude. We expect our students to be open to growth and learning, and it would be an awkward dynamic if, faced with a learning opportunity ourselves, we claimed that we were "too old to learn new things" or suggested that we were unable to learn because our intelligence was predetermined. In order to cultivate this mindset, we need to first be aware of our capabilities and remain open to improving.

Freire (1998) teaches us:

> My security does not rest on the false supposition that I know everything or that I am the "greatest." On the contrary, it rests on the conviction that there are some things I know and some things I do not know. With this conviction it is more likely that I may come to know better what I already know and better learn what I do not yet know. My security is grounded on the knowledge, which experience itself confirms, that I am unfinished.
>
> (p. 120)

Like many other skills we discuss in this book, we should aim to embrace a growth mindset, model it for students, *and* provide opportunities for students to cultivate the skill themselves. Each of us and a number of our colleagues have explicitly discussed having a growth mindset with our students. It makes a great lesson for the start of the year or in preparation for assessments. There are a number of excellent TED Talks that can inspire discussion. Another method is to have students transform fixed mindset statements into ones that demonstrate a growth mindset. It is a powerful and motivating feeling to go from "I can't do that" to "I can't do that *yet*."

Exploring Our Own Identities, Privileges, and Disadvantages

As we discuss self-awareness and areas for growth, it is also important to recognize our own identities and how they shape our self-views and our interactions with others. Are we aware of our own identities? Do we accept or hide any of our identities? Do we have an understanding of how others view us? Do we have trouble relating to those who identify differently from us?

Being comfortable with our identities, while for some may be difficult, is crucial to living in a way that is healthy and invites authentic interactions with others. True, some of our identities may not be visible and we may not choose to acknowledge or discuss them with students, but we ideally should be in a place where we feel comfortable in our own skin. Without this self-acceptance, it becomes difficult to identify our own areas for growth and to model this for students.

While some of our identities may stand out as the most important in our lives, it is also useful to understand how others see us, and whether that matches our self-view. It may not, and that may not necessarily be problematic, but it should provide us with key insight into how to better build relationships moving forward. Maybe we are unaware of, or do not closely identify with, an identity in which we may access privilege because we are not forced to confront it as often as others may.

Note: We suggest that you pause here and complete the first reflective activity below. We will now discuss the recognition of our identities and it may be useful to first reflect upon your own before continuing.

As Tatum (1997/2003) discusses, when asked to complete the sentence "I am _____," individuals who are members of dominant or advantaged social groups often do not mention these identities. Instead, "the parts of our identity that *do* capture our attention are those that other people notice, and that reflect back to us" (p. 20). This has also been true in Val's experiences discussing identity with both students and other educators. If, in their everyday lives, individuals feel like the "other" in some aspect of their identity, they more readily acknowledge this identity as opposed to other aspects of themselves.

We would argue that conscious attention should be paid to each of our identities, regardless of whether they are noticed by outsiders, because they are important for understanding all the parts of our individual selves and our interactions with others. Accepting our identities will also tie into accepting the societal privileges and disadvantages of each identity. The level of privilege we may experience will depend on many factors, importantly our location and the intersectionality of our identities. In order to best understand how we fit into our communities and relationships within those communities, we need to acknowledge how privilege and disadvantage impact us. The first step is acknowledging our identities.

VK: Certain experiences may pull us into greater self-awareness of our privileges. Until I had my children and began using a stroller daily, I had not fully recognized my privilege as an able-bodied person who can step and move freely using my legs. Having never had much difficulty navigating a thin sidewalk or entryway or stepping over thresholds, I had not considered just how much my able-bodiedness impacted my daily life. While the ADA requires public facilities to be wheelchair accessible, even with a stroller with wheels that I can lift, I found many places labeled "accessible" to be functionally inaccessible. In fact, I visited an "accessible" museum last week that had elevators and ramps but entryway thresholds so high that they could not be rolled over without physically lifting one's wheels. I know this because another woman and I had difficulty navigating the hallway – in both cases, wheel lifts (stroller and wheelchair) were needed. While I don't yet know the full challenges of those who use wheelchairs, I have a better understanding of my able-bodied privilege now that my attention has been drawn to it.

Experiences and events can draw our attention to such advantages in our lives but we can also try our best to acknowledge these without such things occurring. Again, reflective exercises can be helpful in alerting us to see what may not be visible. Doing an internet search for "wheel of privilege" will provide a number of diagrams that can help us to think about ways in which we may access power and privilege. Do these areas relate to the ways in which we self-identify? Do we tend to identify more strongly in the categories for which we may experience less privilege? How do our levels of power and privilege help us to relate to others or distance us from others? Knowing the answers to these questions can help us to better know ourselves and how we may, knowingly or unknowingly, relate to others and how others relate to us.

Ricketts (2021), in her book *Do Better*, discusses the importance of understanding the power and privilege of whiteness. She explains that many white people "wander through life unaware of their whiteness and the ways in which they benefit from and perpetuate white supremacy on the daily, resulting in chronic acts of unintentional violence toward BI&PoC" (p. 70). She also acknowledges that the easy accessibility of information has effectively made this way of being an "intentional act." But, as she writes, "your privilege-cloaked whiteness protected you from bringing this information into your consciousness. From needing to know" (pp. 70–71). It is the *awareness* of the power of unearned privilege that is important, as the recognition of a problem is necessary for any solution to be explored.

Students, too, can be encouraged to explore their identities and privileges through intentional lesson activities. As an example, one of the assessment options for the "inequality" unit of Val's elective course was an "Awareness Challenge" that tasked students with keeping a daily journal in which they acknowledged ten privileges or disadvantages they had encountered in their own lives. The immediate goal was to bring awareness to the daily ways in which Americans encounter both privileges and disadvantages. The ultimate goal though was to normalize the *recognition* of each of these to help avoid future defensiveness if any such privilege were called out and, more importantly, call out disadvantage when it is observed. This activity helped students, many for the first time, reflect upon the ways in which their access to fresh produce, their non-accented English, or the daily use of a vehicle fundamentally changed their lives.

While discussing privilege may be difficult for some, there are strategies to help. Some of these stress-reducing strategies will be discussed more in-depth in Chapter 9. Val has found, working with adults and teenagers, that having each person identify a way in which they experience privilege and a way in which they experience disadvantage (the wheel of privilege can be useful here) helps promote conversation and allows for relatability among discussion participants. Allowing space for open dialogue and personal experiences to be shared can also help participants to realize disadvantages that they may not have considered before.

Phillips and Lowery (2015), when researching the natural inclination to deny a claim that a person's privilege is unearned, found strategies to lessen the tendency to deny privilege. When first reminded of their accomplishments, research participants more readily accepted the assertion of their particular privileged place in society. Rather than becoming defensive about our positions of privilege, we can remind ourselves of our accomplishments to better appreciate both the advantages and disadvantages we have experienced. This strategy may be especially useful for educational leaders to keep in mind when facilitating professional development related to privilege and equity.

The Role of Neuroplasticity

A helpful reminder at this point is that any aspects of our behavior that we uncover to be disadvantageous to relationship-building can be changed. Our brains are ever-changing and allow for this to occur through commitment and practice.

KMH: I used to have a negative view of students who cut my class. It rarely happens, but when it does, it is always kind of a shock. With this particular student, instead of getting angry or writing her up, I decided to take the approach of being concerned. Even though I could feel my ego pricked, I made an active and energetic choice to concern myself with her safety instead of her rule-breaking. (This is important here because I have been intentionally experimenting with a new way of being.) I have been trained by administrators and fellow teachers alike to approach students who break the rules with the "no nonsense" method: someone does something that isn't allowed, you punish them, they fear you, they remember the consequences, and they will hesitate to do the same thing again. But this does not take into account any of what the student is experiencing or what the consequence is doing to the future of your STR. Also, it is the *antithesis* of restorative.

In this particular case, our STR was already quite fragile. I was feeling low trust and low engagement from this student. The day she decided to cut class for 15 minutes was a day I wasn't feeling close to her yet. I had a very clear understanding that this was my *one* chance to show her she was precious to me. Even though I wasn't yet trusting of her or endeared to her very much, I decided to take the chance. Many months later (yesterday), this student revealed that my having shown caring and loving concern rather than anger that day allowed her to realize she was safe with me. That day she decided she could trust me, and she wanted to have a good strong relationship with me. So, it worked. I learned that making a choice to be kind was the right move.

The reason I was able to make the choice to try a different approach and new response is because the brain is neuroplastic – it changes in response to experience. When you understand the neuroplasticity of the brain at a biological level, it becomes even more palpable. Science is showing us that neurons (brain cells) continually build new dendritic connections to the synaptic terminals of other neurons all the time, until the moments before death. In simpler terms, this means that the dendrites (the "fingers" of the neurons reaching out to receive information) make new connections to the axons (the message-senders from other neurons). Because of the brain's tendency to constantly rewire, we reshape our brains daily. This means we can learn forever, and *can* change our beliefs. This means a level of learning and unlearning is achievable that we never thought possible before.

I saw a video a couple of decades ago showing that terminally ill patients were growing new dendrites up until the moment of death. I saw the image of dendrites, in green, lit up on a screen, and they were physically *growing*. That was an eye-opening experience for me. I realized that this must happen at the biological level for every human, from birth until death. This new knowledge – that neuroplasticity is universal – changed my thinking about teaching and learning.

Because of this ability to build and rebuild our brains, we know that our "natural" behaviors can be changed. So feel free to remind that uncle who always claims on holidays that he is too old to change his thinking. As we will discuss more fully in Chapter 9, we can self-regulate and ultimately lower our stress levels by doing so. But, first, we need to stop and notice what is happening.

Benefits of Increasing Self-Awareness

Pattakos and Dundon (2017), reflecting on Viktor Frankl's writing, use the following unattributed quote, "Between stimulus and response there is a space. In that space is our power to choose our response. In our response lies our growth and our freedom" (p. VI).

So then our goal becomes: I n c r e a s e   t h e   s p a c e.

Brackett (2019) suggests the use of a "Meta-Moment" to allow for acknowledgment of this space.

> In simplest terms, it's a pause. The Meta-Moment involves hitting the brakes and stepping out of time…. Taking one or more deep breaths may also be a part of it. Anything to give ourselves a little room to maneuver and deactivate.
>
> (p. 158)

This space allows us to be open to new ideas. Learning that this space is real can be the first step to increasing our self-awareness. Since we increasingly live in a more digitally dominant world, it is worth reminding ourselves how absent the space can be. Consider the examples of replying to a social media post without thinking about the level of appropriateness or clicking to continue to the next episode of a show on Netflix as opposed to getting more sleep.

Increasing our self-awareness can then help us to exert greater self-control. In *Self-Reg*, Shanker (2017) offers five steps that we can practice. In an effort to give her students the gift of self-regulation and to encourage it in herself, Kate teaches these steps over the course of the academic year. First, they read the signs of how they are behaving and reframe their actions. Then they identify the stressors, find ways to reduce the stress (within our spheres of control), and reflect.

Just reflecting on the stressors that cause our behaviors becomes a powerful way to gain control within our lives. Then we can *respond*. We respond to the entire process by figuring out what helps us calm, rest, and recover, and we do this so that we have the time, the space, and the capacity to respond, rather than react. For, with reaction, there is no pause. With the acknowledgment of the *space* – which can only come with self-awareness and the practice of self-awareness – comes the ability to make a choice. Control is the ability to choose. When we control, we possess the power to decide, the power to withdraw, the power to move forward, the power to abstain, the power to be silent, and the power to rise up.

Milkman and Duckworth (2021) also discuss the importance of our self-awareness. They explain how "our beliefs can redirect our attention" and also affect our physiology directly (p. 157). In the field of behavioral psychology, scientists are finding physical evidence that our thoughts have neuroendocrine repercussions.

The benefits of being self-aware extend to many aspects of our teaching including teaching during difficult times in our own personal lives. It is difficult to teach after a traumatic event, a loss, an extended illness, or a break-up. It's difficult to do anything, really.

> VK: As a person who tends to avoid the discomfort of facing reality when something bad happens, I find comfort in the distraction of teaching. I now recognize that avoidance of emotions ultimately is not the healthiest choice and that voicing my emotions more often, allowing for the validation and support of others, is a better method to get through the sadness or frustration. Sharing my losses, frustrations, and other difficult aspects of being human with my students, although awkward at first, helped to show students my truth and provided opportunities to connect with students facing similar circumstances. While I didn't want to pass on my grief to the students, a simple "I may seem off today and this is why…and this is how I feel…" at the beginning of class let them know and made me feel less pressure to "act normal" when I didn't feel "normal." This is not to be confused with using students as a source of emotional support; instead, it served as a way to put them at ease when my behaviors didn't match my usual way of being.

Practicing identifying and naming emotions can be helpful in several ways. It can allow for a greater understanding and control over the physical bodily responses experienced during various emotions. Understanding the physical changes associated with the beginning of an emotion can also help to plan one's response to it, which is especially useful when standing in front of a group. Modeling this practice and assisting students in naming emotions is also a beneficial classroom practice, especially for students who have difficulty with emotional regulation. For younger students, using a basic emotion wheel or color chart may be helpful, and for older students, the more detailed emotion wheel may be useful and provide an opportunity to discuss the emotions in more detail, referencing the outermost circle on the wheel.

Freire (1970/2018) reminds us, "Those who authentically commit themselves to the people must re-examine themselves constantly" (p. 60). We believe that this re-examination is an obligation of anyone who works with others in a mentorship capacity. Beyond that, we also know that it will improve *our* lives. Intentional focus on bringing greater self-awareness allows for the identification of areas to grow, improving relationships, and ultimately decreasing stress, and can serve as a way to process emotions.

This is why increasing opportunities to recognize where one might need to change is so important. We have already discussed how feedback can be powerful in helping us to identify these areas. As reflective educators, we need to seek opportunities to be "pulled up short" (Kerdeman, 2003). When we are "pulled up short," we are forced to face something about ourselves or the world we haven't considered before, something that surprises us. Often this can be a question from a student or a comment from a colleague. It can also be a sentence in a book (maybe this book!) or an Instagram post. This openness to facing new, and sometimes unsettling, knowledge and perspectives only helps us to grow.

Wilson (2002) discusses in the aptly named book *Strangers to Ourselves* how so much of our minds – our thinking and behaviors – are outside of our consciousness. Because of this, he suggests that "it is often better to *deduce* the nature of our hidden minds by looking outward at our behavior and how others react to us" (p. 16). Essentially, we need others to help us to learn about ourselves. In the next chapter, we will discuss ways to best use the feedback of others in our communities to assist in our self-awareness journeys.

Reflective Activities

- Make a list of your personal identities. Which of these identities do you think about most often? Why?

- Ask a friend or colleague to share how they view you. Does their perceived view of you match the way in which you identify?

- Consider a recent professional experience in which you felt profound emotion. Did you acknowledge the specific emotions you felt? Looking back, can you identify and label these specific emotions? If not, locate an emotion wheel online and consider making it a habit to label and express your emotions in order to increase your ability to self-regulate.
- To what extent do you find it difficult to identify the emotions of others? (You can test this by guessing the emotions of a colleague or trusted friend.) Are there particular emotions that are more difficult for you to identify? What are some ways you can build your skill in reading these emotions?

- Consider and discuss how you feel when you discover an area where you could improve. Does your response represent a growth mindset? If not, how can you reframe your response to represent a growth mindset?

- Ask a friend or colleague how you make them feel. Does their response match your intention for your way of being?

References

Brackett, M. (2019). *Permission to feel: The power of emotional intelligence to achieve well-being and success.* New York: Celadon Books.

Dweck, C. S. (2007). *Mindset: The new psychology of success.* New York: Ballantine Books.

Ekman, P. (2007). *Emotions revealed: Recognizing faces and feelings to improve communication and emotional life.* New York: Macmillan.

Freire, P. (1998). *Pedagogy of freedom: Ethics, democracy, and civic courage.* Lanham, MD: Rowman & Littlefield Publishers.

Freire, P. (1970/2018). *Pedagogy of the oppressed.* New York: Bloomsbury.

hooks, b. (1994). *Teaching to transgress: Education as the practice of freedom.* London: Routledge.

Jans-Beken, J., Jacobs, N., Janssens, M., Peeters, S., Reijnders, J., Lechner, L., & Lataster, J. (2019). Gratitude and health: An updated review. *The Journal of Positive Psychology.* https://doi.org/10.1080/17439760.2019.1651888

Kerdeman, D. (2003). Pulled up short: Challenging self-understanding as a focus of teaching and learning. *Journal of Philosophy of Education, 37*(2), 293–308.

Milkman, K. L., & Duckworth, A. (2021). *How to change: The science of getting from where you are to where you want to be.* New York: Portfolio/Penguin.

Nhất Hạnh, T. (2001/2009). *You are here: Discovering the magic of the present moment.* Boulder, CO: Shambhala Publications.

Pattakos, A., & Dundon, E. (2017). *Prisoners of our thoughts.* Oakland, CA: Berrett-Koehler Publishers.

Phillips, L. T., & Lowery, B. S. (2015). The hard-knock life? Whites claim hardships in response to racial inequity. *Journal of Experimental Social Psychology, 61,* 12–18.

Ricketts, R. (2021). *Do better: Spiritual activism for fighting and healing from white supremacy.* New York: Simon & Schuster.

Shanker, S. (2017). *Self-reg: How to help your child (and you) break the stress cycle and successfully engage with life.* New York: Penguin Press.

Tatum, B. D. (1997/2003). *"Why are all the Black kids sitting together in the cafeteria?" and other conversations about race.* New York: Basic Books.

Tolle, E. (1999/2004). *The power of now.* Vancouver, BC, Canada: Namaste Publishing.

Wilson, T. D. (2002). *Strangers to ourselves: Discovering the adaptive unconscious.* Cambridge, MA & London, England: The Belknap Press of Harvard University Press.

7

Establishing Effective Working Relationships and Utilizing Accountability Partners

How Collegial Relationships Improve Our Teaching

Teaching is tough. Managing the emotions of children is tough. Receiving feedback is tough. Reflecting on our actions and biases is tough. We will have times when we need to lean on others, especially those who understand the pressures of the job. In this chapter, we will first explore the reasons why supportive collegial relationships are the backbone of an educator's self-care and social and emotional well-being. We recognize that not all collegial relationships become full-fledged friendships, but we maintain that teacher-friendships are the most transformative of all, when it is possible for them to form.

Benefits of Collegial Relationships

We strongly believe that having a trusting teacher pod is essential to sustaining life as an educator in a way that is healthy and successful for both ourselves and the students we serve. Neither of us can imagine how much more difficult our teaching careers would have been, had we not had our lunch table crew and trusted teacher-friends to bounce ideas off of, to cry with after receiving negative feedback, to question our biases, to vent, and to bring sunshine to a stormy teaching day. Knowing that we could talk to one of these loving people before leaving the workday meant that we would leave with less stress. It is invaluable to know that others have experienced the same, or very similar, difficulties and can provide suggestions, solutions, and/or a hug.

On top of the emotional benefit of teacher collegiality, these relationships undoubtedly have improved our teaching practice. We have teacher-friends who we can count on to suggest resources or lesson ideas when we are stuck and know that they expect nothing in return. We have others with whom we share the same teaching goals and those who, having already established prior relationships with our students, can provide insight to help us build connections with them. Even just telling stories during class about experiences with colleagues outside of the school day has functioned as a means for bonding authentically with our students. In so many ways, our interactions and our friendships with colleagues have resulted in personal and professional growth, which consequently have improved our abilities to best serve our students.

As Kate has acknowledged, the light of self-scrutiny can be too bright in the absence of friendship. But the safety of friendship allows it to be less blinding, less jarring. It is in the loving arms of a friend, who is a teacher too, that we are able to see ourselves as we truly are, and not be paralyzed with shame. We are, instead, safe to shed the layers of self-judgment and self-reproach to reveal a truer version of ourselves.

Val clearly remembers her purposeful avoidance of colleagues during her first year of teaching. Like any new teacher, she felt overwhelmed by the work and wanted to spend all her time planning or grading, saving her social and emotional energy for the students. She stuck with pleasant greetings and small talk and hid away when she could. A few of her colleagues insisted that she be more social and, at the very least, join for lunch. Despite feeling like she had no energy to talk *more* during the day, she did. They were right; she needed the socialization and the venting space. She needed the lunch table.

We recognize that we have been lucky to develop so many of these mutually beneficial relationships in our teaching careers and that all may not have the same opportunity. We would suggest to those that are limited in their interactions with colleagues to look online and find forums of teachers who share the same teaching goals. Many of the larger teacher organizations have subgroups in which one can find educators representing diverse content specialties, teaching styles, and identity groups. This is a profession of community, and we need to nurture that.

Our friendship, which has led to the writing of this book, serves as a great example of what can come of developing effective working relationships and friendships with colleagues. As we began to share more of both our professional and personal experiences, we found that we could help one another to better achieve our goals through shared reflection. We began to realize the important connections between the topics we each taught – biology and social issues – and recognized how this knowledge could improve our teaching.

KMH: I'm writing this book because Val Kearns decided she liked me enough to room with me in Italy when we chaperoned a school orchestra trip together in November 2014. Then we got locked out of a big old castle and stood shivering and hungry at the door. She decided she liked who I was and, of course, I adored her immediately. Now, here we are trying to capture on paper all the years of classroom experience that can be distilled for the lessons and the wisdom they hold.

My associations now are carefully chosen and lead to places that offer hope, growth, and love. Every time I hear Val speak or read her writing, I know she believes what I believe. Val has taught me to step back, detach, and lovingly look for the root cause of a human's behavior. In fact, Val will explain to you the actions of anyone, and if she cannot, she will dig deeply until she can find an explanation of their behavior, words, actions, choices, and, ultimately, beliefs. This friendship with Val has shaped me in the most incredible way, teaching me to suspend judgment and really anchor myself in compassion and love. And like my mother, and like any truly good and talented teacher, Val believes in me and my capacity for good.

VK: Kate and I met as teachers. While I can't remember the exact moment we met, I know I felt an instant warmth from her and knew she was a source of comfort in the building. I'm not surprised that this connection developed into a lifelong friendship, cemented by our chaperoning adventures in Italy, our overlapping pregnancies, and the pumping closet we shared. She is a person who shares the same goals of personal growth and will provide honest, thoughtful feedback for any situation I bring to her. She has helped me to achieve many of my career goals, including writing this book. She has provided genuine encouragement and motivation that has propelled me to work harder toward my goals and to set ones I hadn't known that I wanted to achieve. I know she does this for each of her students, too. Not only does she help people around her to see their own light, but she also lends her light, making theirs brighter.

This type of trusted colleague is one we can ask to check us on our unconscious behaviors and monitor our language to ensure inclusivity. For us, we can hold one another accountable and know that there is no judgment since we have the same goals – to better ourselves and to better connect with others for the greater purpose of bettering our communities. We can correct one another's incorrect pronunciation of a student's name and remind each other not to refer to a group of people as "guys." We can role-play a scenario if one is feeling stressed about an encounter with a student or supervisor. We can have one another read and edit a response email to ensure the communication is received as intended. In short, we are able to make our professional burdens and teaching loads less heavy through our interactions and mutual support.

Suggested Debriefing Protocol (5F and 5G Framework)

We want to share our process for debriefing difficult experiences as an example of a protocol that can be used in informal or formal settings. We developed this process when recognizing that our shared Marco Polo video chats with another dear friend served as a space for meaningful personal and professional reflection. After one of our Zoom writing calls where we brainstormed the process of debriefing with a friend, we created this framework out of our ideas, which we call the 5F and 5G "Feel Good" Framework.

Guidelines:	No expectations
	No judgment
	Confidentiality
Person 1:	**Find:** <u>F</u>ind a safe space or private place (digital or physical)
	Feel: How do you <u>f</u>eel in this moment?
	Facts: <u>F</u>acts as you remember them
	Feedback: Sharing <u>f</u>eedback already received from others (if any)
	Forward: Your reflection/options you have considered moving <u>f</u>orward
Person 2:	**Gratitude:** Expression of gratitude
	Give: <u>G</u>iving a summary
	Growth: Acknowledging observations about areas of <u>g</u>rowth and strength
	Gauge: <u>G</u>auging the degree of bias (negativity, personal)
	Generate: <u>G</u>enerating questions for continued reflection

Since we developed this process based on video chats, it allowed each person to take the time to fully listen, replay if necessary, and then provide a response, all without interruption. It allows for the *space* for more deliberate reflection while listening fully to the other. In the absence of video chats, we can recreate that space by minimizing interruption as "Person 1" shares their experience. Beyond debriefing a difficult situation, this process can also be used in cases of conflict or situations where colleagues need to repair a working relationship. We have also used this protocol to support one another in developing and progressing toward a particular goal, effectively serving as accountability partners.

Teaching is one of those jobs that requires a full emotional investment, which can be difficult for someone in another profession to understand, as much as they may care about us and want to support us. While someone outside of the profession can certainly serve as an accountability partner and source of support, they would need to understand why it's so important that we send that email *right now* as opposed to in the morning.

Methods to Encourage Professional Collaborative Learning

Many schools and districts have worked to establish collaborative learning opportunities, often through structured professional learning communities, or PLCs. While a highly structured program might successfully meet the needs of teachers, fewer administrative constraints can also be effective and can allow for more organic partnerships to form. In these cases, as Kruse, Louis, and Bryk (1994) discuss, administrative support is still necessary to support a healthy professional culture. This support should include both structural conditions (such as time to meet and talk, physical proximity, interdependent teaching roles, and ensuring communication structures) *and* social and human resources (such as openness to improvement, demonstration of respect and trust, and ensuring teachers have expertise in the knowledge and skills of teaching). These points may be particularly useful for educators in leadership roles, as well as administrators who want to be sensitive to the needs of their teachers.

We have experienced administrator support and encouragement of collegial partnerships as part of the required yearly teacher evaluation process. Our district allowed teachers to participate in an Alternative Evaluation program that provided this opportunity. We suggest that educators seek out supportive administration when possible to advocate for these types of experiences, as this program was a crucial piece in our learning process as educators.

Val feels fortunate to have worked with a beloved colleague, Erin Schomburg, to identify specific problems of practice and work throughout the year, documenting data and meeting to discuss strategies for implementation to address these problems. They observed one another's classes and met together at various points during the year to discuss their efforts in increasing student voice and choice and maximizing opportunities for authentic civic engagement. Because they shared the same goals of increasing youth critical consciousness and civic engagement, they were able to bounce ideas off one another in a way that challenged and promoted thinking. They were also able to provide useful suggestions that were relatable and practical. These suggestions were both content-specific and goal-oriented, such as a possible authentic audience for an upcoming assessment, the rewording of a discussion question to better relate to student lives and communities, or a restructuring option for an activity to promote increased participation.

The ability to have those conversations and reflect helped to reshape their lessons and assessments in ways that captured greater student engagement and led to increased civic participation of the students. This model of observing and reflecting with a peer on a project based on a shared goal allowed for meaningful change to be made in each of their classrooms within a single academic school year. For each of them, increasing democratic practices in various ways in the classroom resulted in increased student engagement in *all* aspects of class. Based on their success, they chose to continue this project for the next two years, fine-tuning and reworking based on student feedback and data. This level of reflection resulting in meaningful change would not have been possible through the traditional observation model in which observers often have little content knowledge or familiarity with the teacher's style and goals in the classroom.

Kate has also participated in this program with Jen Bridgewater, a colleague in her department. Having taught together for nearly ten years, they came to the point where they realized that the most important skill upon which their friendship as teachers rests was their ability to share ideas. They realized that they could identify habits of mind, such as listening and sharing, and teach them to their students, as many who are doing the cutting-edge research in social and emotional learning (SEL) are doing. In the context of individual metacognitive practices, which they have been using in their teaching for several years now, they decided to teach mini-lessons on self-awareness, empathy, self-regulation, and listening, to name a few.

In what they call their "Quest for Synchronicity," they pioneered their own way of brainstorming that allowed them to tap into the brilliance of the other in a way that they could replicate for their students. This led to their development of a metacognitive process of peer evaluation that has become a brain-changing experience for each of them and their students. They realized that, as their ability to both highlight and teach self-awareness increased; they saw that the process alone was causing a heightened level of reported empathy by students in their metacognitive notes. This discovery solidified for them that there is no more important set of skills than the interpersonal ones we first teach at the lower levels in school. As time goes on, as students get older and the material and content burgeons, these skills are assumed to be present but are rarely taught explicitly again at the middle and high school levels. Their work has brought this into focus and fully integrated socio-emotional learning back into their high school science classrooms.

As part of the project, they observed one another's teaching. Through this observation process, Kate was able to see how Jen uses language powerfully to weave lessons about being human into her teaching about how the forces of the universe work. For example, in one lesson she made a pun about the No (abbreviation for normal) force: "It's not the No force, but the force of No is powerful. No means no."

Kate was also able to observe Jen's interactions with each person in the room and noted how these interactions were based on the exact level each student needed. As we have mentioned throughout the book, modeling behaviors for our students can serve as some of the most meaningful lessons for students.

Jen has an intuitive grasp of the amount of attention and explanation each student requires. She possesses a heightened self-awareness which affords her the ability to observe, notice, and be fully aware and present. Jen concluded her teacher-directed part of the lesson mentioned previously with these words: "This is your time to shine. We spend a lot of time building the foundation…." These two concepts perfectly summed up Kate and Jen's work together: in allowing students to grow and succeed in the emotionally safe learning environments they carefully and intentionally created in their classrooms, they helped build foundational habits that will serve the students in their future learning and professional careers.

They collected metacognitive thinking data that included self-reflection and that extended to collaborative sharing about the learning experience and the metacognition that ensued. They made the choice to focus on this type of data after realizing that in *their* metacognitive work during their teaching careers, the focus had been on the individual's thinking. This encouraged individualism and did little to directly foster empathy. Also, it kept the individual learning about their own thinking in isolation. Instead, in this project, they decided to simply extend student metacognitive notes into a format that included a section based solely on collaboration about thinking. Students completed their own summaries about the choices they made, the learning journeys they took as a result, and the thoughts and conclusions they had about it. Then they shared with a peer on a somewhat regular basis. They culled the most useful data for answering their focus question: How can students increase self-awareness and self-regulation when they regularly engage in self- and peer-evaluation discussions? In other words, how does collaborative metacognition increase self-awareness?

This Alternative Evaluation program allowed for the opportunity for each of us to tackle projects that we had wanted to address but could not find the time amidst the avalanche of teacher demands. Once realizing that completing this project took the place of some of those demands, it became attainable, and enjoyable, for each of us to complete. While many districts or states may not be able to implement such a program, a similar project could be used in place of existing tasks, maybe having more targeted yearly reflections or faculty meetings that aim to partner faculty with similar goals. Fostering these collegial partnerships creates a lower-stress environment for teachers and ultimately for students, as a more secure and healthy teacher will be better able to provide for the needs of their students.

Identifying and Capitalizing on Individual Strengths in Collegial Projects

In our working process for writing this book, we have understood that the recognition and utilization of the strengths and learning styles of each participant are key for expediting a project (a book, curriculum writing, lesson planning, etc.) and maximizing its potential. We are sure that many of our readers can think back to a curriculum writing experience with unfamiliar colleagues that seemed to take forever. As we think back on these experiences, we each may recognize that these projects became difficult because we were not able to effectively build on the strengths of each participant. We suggest that when individuals are chosen for professional projects that the project coordinators consider interpersonal relationships and the number of participants. This will allow for people to bring their best to the table, rather than feeling the discomfort that can result in withdrawal or focusing on efficiency rather than quality.

To help identify a person's strengths, we can first look to identify how they learn and process information. Some ways to determine this might include asking someone questions like:

- How do you read?
- How do you learn material in a classroom?
- How do you plan to make a speech or write an essay?

In our case, Kate prefers to learn in an auditory way and is a poetic writer, while Val prefers learning visually and tends to condense writing into concise ideas. As a result, we work effectively when Kate listens to Val reading aloud and formulates new ideas, adding detail and locating words, while Val writes. Val then edits and summarizes the writing. Interestingly, this also relates to our interaction styles – Val tends to notice the big picture (e.g. whole face) while Kate focuses on details (e.g. freckles, the shape of a nose or chin).

Having information about the ways in which a person best learns and produces work can help to better organize a project. *Then* groupings and particular tasks can be distributed based on areas of expertise and interest. Often, the first step is missing and colleagues just choose areas to work without first understanding how the work can be more collaborative and how each person can best contribute. Yes, this method will take longer, but it will ultimately be a better product. Administrators can help to encourage and support such experiences by building in time to allow for greater planning and structuring before beginning a project.

Feedback and Accountability in Working Relationships

Because of the deep respect Val and Kate have for one another, our willingness to receive feedback is ever-present and, as a result, we are easily able to provide critical feedback on one another's individual writing. Kate can tell Val, "There are too many ideas in that single sentence" or "There is no emotion in your writing here" and Val can tell Kate, "You already said that" or "That's too personal."

We provide this feedback in our personal lives as well as our professional lives, helping to hold one another accountable in our life goals. Each of us greatly values the other for fulfilling this role as well as the other individuals in our lives who are able to give us feedback that helps us to grow. However, this is often a difficult role to fill for another as receiving and providing unlovely feedback can be uncomfortable, as we discuss in Chapter 5. The feedback becomes much easier to both give and receive, though, when it is tied to a stated goal. For example, if Val tells her partner that she wants to start going to bed earlier, it should be easier for him to talk about the uselessness of watching yet another episode of *90 Day Fiancé* and how it is impeding her writing progress. (But, really, what better way to study human beings and the nuances of relationships?!) Rather than feeling judged by him for exposing her brain to such material, she might recognize that he is helping to hold her accountable to her goal.

Similarly, we can use our collegial relationships to hold us accountable in ways that feel affirming and purposeful. Administrators can help to create opportunities for faculty – encouraging partner work in the same department or self-selected partnerships – to discuss professional goals and specific areas to receive feedback. When we can enlist help to achieve our goals, we can feel empowered, rather than judged, when we receive feedback.

Acknowledging behaviors that detract from our goals should be addressed if we want to achieve them. Since it may be difficult for us to notice these behaviors on our own, we can utilize others in an effort to help us grow. An important factor here is the expressed willingness to receive feedback. We have found that the absence of this explicit consent to receive feedback results in the unnecessary continuing of unconscious behaviors and, in many cases, unnecessary discomfort on the part of the observer. The use of accountability partners becomes especially helpful as we discuss bias in the next chapter, as most of our biases play out in unconscious ways.

A sense of collegiality is crucial in our work, for ourselves, and ultimately for our students. Supportive collegial relationships play a vital role in promoting teacher professional growth, job satisfaction, and professional commitment as well as improving measures of school quality and student performance (Shah, 2012). They serve as emotional sanctuaries for *us* as we hope our classrooms serve as emotional sanctuaries for our students. They are effectively *our* classrooms, and we need to create and foster them as spaces that allow for thriving.

Reflective Activities

- Identify those you confide in regarding professional difficulties. Why do you choose these individuals? What qualities about each person make them a good (or not so good) person to confide in?

- Select one aspect of your communication (verbal or nonverbal) that you want to improve. Which of your colleagues shares this goal? Who or what can hold you accountable in achieving this goal?

- Think of a recent challenge in your professional life. Practice the sharing protocol (5F and 5G Framework) discussed above with a partner. Reflect on your feelings about the process afterward and whether it feels different or helpful to share in this way.

- Identify your own strengths in a collaborative group project. What is your process to reach a predetermined goal? How do you personally best contribute to a shared task?

- Consider the experience of receiving constructive criticism from someone in your personal or professional life. Did this feedback feel like an attempt to hold you accountable or was it merely judgmental? Now, consider recent constructive criticism you provided for another. Was this feedback an attempt to hold them accountable or was it merely judgmental? How could each of these experiences have been improved?

References

Kruse, S., Louis, K. S., & Bryk, A. (Spring 1994). Building professional community in schools. *Issues in Restructuring Schools*, (6): 3–6.

Shah, M. (2012). The importance and benefits of teacher collegiality in schools – A literature review. *Procedia-Social and Behavioral Sciences, 46*, 1242–1246.

8

Confronting Bias

How to Identify, Reflect Upon, and Combat Types of Bias that Arise in Ourselves and in the Classroom

When reading the title of this chapter, do you notice any physical reactions in your body that may indicate stress? Does discussing bias make you uncomfortable? If it doesn't, great! You likely have realized that all humans have bias and, rather than feeling guilt about it, have come to a place of acceptance. If you do feel stress or discomfort, stick around! We would love to help get you to a place where discussing bias feels less stressful and more empowering.

The Nature of Bias

Let's begin, like many of those who write on this topic, by reminding ourselves that having biases is natural and reflects the human tendency to categorize and survive. Our brains are pre-programmed, thanks to evolution, with shortcuts that allow for faster processing. Many of these shortcuts serve as helpful adaptations in our daily lives, particularly in cases of emergency (Marcus, 2008). We naturally respond to stimuli and categorize, often before we are even aware that we are doing so. For example, we jump back when something falls in front of us because our brains recognize the object as a potential danger.

These categorizations can also apply to people, and this is where our brain's shortcut strategy may become less helpful. These are the forms of bias, those that are unconscious and implicit, that we find most meaningful to address in the way they relate to our professions and daily lives.

Acts indicating preferences for one student or groups of students over another can be one way in which we display our biases. And seemingly demonstrating favoritism can be one of the quickest ways to lose connection with students. While, of course, we may have deeper connections with some students, demonstrating preferential treatment for these students, or even seemingly doing so, will result in an unwinding of any sense of community for those not on the receiving end of this treatment. This is not to say that each student should not be acknowledged for their individual strengths or provided attention and assistance according to their need. The problem arises when students do not feel as valued as they perceive these "preferred" student/s to be. Rather, the students who are not "preferred" may understand the disadvantages that are accruing over time as they are shortchanged the time and attention they deserve.

Intentional communication with students is a simple way to address situations where a teacher may be providing more attention to, or seemingly showing favoritism toward, others. This can come in the form of positive validation of each student for their individual strengths or explicit reminders that each student has different strengths and needs and, accordingly, will need more or less of our attention throughout the year. It can also be a direct acknowledgment that we have known that student's family for years and are able to joke with them since we have a greater sense of familiarity. As we have discussed in earlier chapters, transparency in our actions helps to build trust and prevents potential perceptions of favoritism.

Examples of perceived favoritism noted by Val's former students include the following:

- More frequent attention in terms of calling on a student or having longer side conversations compared to other students
- Allowance for late assignments while others are not afforded this privilege
- Allowance for – or less punishment for – common misbehaviors (e.g. phone use, talking)
- Overlooking or excusing more serious misbehaviors (e.g. cutting class)
- Perceived leniency in grading

A number of students also identified teacher "favorites" by recognizing the students who were seemingly ignored by the teacher, effectively the "non-favorites." If students see that others are gaining privileges, while some are disadvantaged respectively in those areas, they will naturally lose trust in the teacher. The lack of trust stemming from inequity aversion, a trend interestingly also exhibited in chimps and capuchins, will likely result in a distancing from the source of the inequity, which would ultimately prevent full engagement in the classroom community (DeSteno, 2015).

While some of these acts may be intentional, such as having longer conversations with familiar students, unintentional favoring of individuals or groups of students can be more problematic. This will be more difficult to address directly with the students since it remains outside our awareness. We may view this as different than intentional favoritism but, in truth, the impact is the same. Our goal is to learn to self-monitor in a way that brings these behaviors into our conscious thought. Banaji and Greenwald (2016) compare reflective thinking, that which we can identify and voice, to automatic thinking.

> The automatic side of our mind, on the other hand, is a quite different entity. It's a stranger to us. We implicitly *know* something or *feel* a certain way, and often these thoughts and feelings are reflected in our actions too - the difference being that we can't always explain these actions, and they are at times completely at odds with our conscious intentions.
>
> (p. 55)

This disassociation can be seen in those who may routinely perform behaviors suggesting negative characteristics about a particular race of people (e.g. physical distancing, facial expressions, questioning intelligence or authority) but will vehemently argue that they are "not racist!" While they may actually *believe* themselves to be so, their automatic behaviors suggest otherwise, and people respond to these automatic behaviors no differently than our conscious behaviors.

Although it will likely make our readers feel uncomfortable to acknowledge, we all have biases that shape the way we view others. We may not think often about these biases or the impacts they have on the people we interact with on a daily basis, but we should. Take a moment and see what images pop into your head when you think about someone who is "attractive" or someone who is "cool." These images may not make us feel uncomfortable because of the positive labels. But, now, think about another positive label: a "good student." Consider how this image could be detrimental to both the people who "fit" this description and those who do not.

In the case of the label "gifted student," for which teacher nominations are necessary, our brain associations can have demonstrable impacts on a student's potential learning and demographic patterns of privilege. Research has shown that high-achieving Black students are less likely than white students to be nominated by teachers, and female students more likely to be nominated than male students (Barber & Torney-Purta, 2008; Elhoweris, Mutua, Alsheikh, & Holloway, 2005). (Notably, the research was based on responses from primarily white teachers, reflective of educator demographic patterns across the nation.) How can we work to ensure our brains do not maintain categorizations that unfairly provide advantages for some and disadvantages for others?

While we cannot control that certain positive and negative images exist, as negative associations of historically marginalized groups are heavily rooted in popular culture, it *is* our fault if we choose to ignore them. We are culpable when we have this knowledge and don't shift. The first step, as with many other self-improvement goals, is identification followed by intentional work.

McCloskey (2020), in his memoir, acknowledges the meaningful moment in which he discovered his implicit association of Black men with criminality:

> We were comparing notes, and I turned to Joe Ravenell and asked, "By the way, who *was* that black guy screaming at me?"
>
> Joe, who also happens to be African American, got a funny look on his face. "That was Butch Layton. He's white."
>
> I am embarrassed to admit that in my moment of terror my inherent prejudice – prejudice of which I'd never been aware – had flooded my senses. I didn't just have the wrong face; I had the wrong race. This was my first experience with how unreliable eyewitness testimony can be. I had walked into that cell block filled with fear and I had conjured up a face to go with the voice that had unleashed that fear – created that face, in my mind, out of my own prejudice.
>
> (p. 14)

In this case, McCloskey's experience brought him greater awareness of not only himself but also the ways in which implicit biases can negatively impact the criminal justice system.

Recognizing our natural biases is not only helpful but also liberating. We all have likely realized that we are more comfortable with those with whom we share an identity or common interest. This is why we look for commonalities when meeting people for the first time. For example, if we learn that we share a birthday with someone, or that our brothers have the same name, we instantly feel a connection and are likely to treat them in a way that reflects this connection. While this similarity bias may function to help build connections with some, it can also be a mechanism for exclusion. For example, if a person has a name that is unfamiliar to us, we may be less likely to interact with them, call on them in class, or hire them, as has been found by numerous research studies (Bertrand & Mullainathan, 2003; Cotton, O'Neill, & Griffin, 2008; Kline, Rose, & Walters, 2022).

In an educational setting, when other colleagues have likely worked with our incoming students or we are familiar with their older siblings, we may also develop preconceived ideas about students based on these prior experiences. Or maybe we assume that the organized individual who was early to class every day last year will automatically excel (the halo effect). It can be difficult to consider all the reasons that our brains will group and prejudge our students, but it is important to consider how and when this is happening.

As Garrison (1996) notes, "Cultural traditions have us before we have them" (p. 360). Our cultures shape our brains. Certain aspects of our culture – our languages, beliefs, values, norms, food, holidays, clothing, music, media – are familiar to us and they (generally) evoke feelings of comfort and safety. As a result, it can be hard to think about our culture as limiting, because often our life goals and belief systems have arisen and reside within it. This makes it difficult to extricate how we feel and what we know. But when we start to think about our cultures and communities as one of many, rather than the *only*, we can start to increase our perceived value of and comfort with others. The more open and accepting we are, rather than just tolerant, the more we can come to know and love members of so many different cultures. In a place of openness and vulnerability, we can expand our communities with true inclusivity.

VK: I was recently reminded of the study of the Nacirema by a student teacher who used this resource in his class. The study described the rituals of this culture, including the following morning routine:

> The daily body ritual performed by everyone includes a mouth rite. Despite the fact that these people are so punctilious about the care of the mouth, this rite involves a practice which strikes the uninitiated stranger as revolting. It was reported to me that the ritual consists of inserting a small bundle of hog hairs into the mouth, along with certain magical powders, and then moving the bundle in a highly formalized series of gestures.
>
> (Miner, 1956, p. 504)

The description of each ritual of the culture is described in ways that evoke distancing and unfamiliarity, despite its description of common practices of American culture like brushing one's teeth. It serves as a useful reminder that American culture is just one of many (and also comprised of many, salad bowl-style), and practices that may seem bizarre and confusing to some humans are common to others. The more often we consider the normalization of our cultural practices, the more easily we can identify our cultural biases.

Strategies for Connection-Building to Combat Conscious Bias

Acknowledging our natural ability to connect with those with whom we share identities, cultures, and interests can help us to realize the importance of building connections with students with whom we do not share identity groups or obvious interests. For these students, we can make a point to ask about their extracurricular activities or attend an event for a club in which they participate. While this may mean that we are stepping out of our comfort zones, it shows a willingness to enter theirs.

As we discussed in Chapter 1, story-telling on the part of the teacher serves as a place to begin. One doesn't need to have a similarity to connect. We all may not have the same favorite food, but we likely all have food memories. We may not all have two brothers, but we likely all have memorable moments with families. We may have not all grown up on a sheep farm, but we all grew up somewhere. Story-telling creates opportunities for the sharing of ourselves. The possibility for connection is open. Our shared humanity is enough.

Building connections across identities and interests applies to student-student relationships as well. For many years in the classroom, Val had students, on the first day, find similarities with their peers as ways of building connection. While the goal of building connections between peers was important, she began to realize that she needed to celebrate and honor differences more on these early days of class. So she began to have them also search for things that made them unique and something that they would like to learn from a peer. Encouraging student-student sharing, socializing, and storytelling within the context of a lesson can also serve to build community. Every classroom should truly be a place where, as Woodson and López (2018) beautifully write, each person can find in another "something a little like you - and something else so fabulously not quite like you at all."

Strategies to Address Implicit Bias

After understanding and identifying our conscious biases, the real challenge of our commitment to growing as humans is to uncover and address our implicit biases. Accountability partners can be helpful with this process, but they, too, may share some of the very hidden biases that we are looking to uncover. After all, our preference for this person was likely due to in-group bias, even if that similarity was our joint dedication to professional growth.

A useful tool, especially for important and often difficult conversations, is the series of Implicit Association Tests developed by Harvard's Project Implicit which can be found at implicit.harvard.edu. These tests identify the strength of our automatic associations regarding specific groups of people and indicate the existence of potential negative biases. We highly recommend exploring this tool and debriefing with trusted friends and colleagues. At the very least, this tool is useful for provoking meaningful conversations about biases and their impacts. At best, this can be a tool to help people to address negative biases and improve their interactions with others. But what can we do about the biases we discover?

In response to the frequently asked question "What can I do about an implicit preference that I don't want?," Project Implicit (2011) suggests:

> There is a large body of evidence suggesting that information that we encounter in the moment (for example, reading a story about a heroic Black person and an immoral White person) can, at least temporarily, shift implicit preferences. However, whether these momentary changes can translate into long-term change in implicit bias is not yet well-established.
>
> If you want to durably change implicit preferences, a quick five-minute intervention may not be enough. Instead, you may have to become more selective about the types of information you consume in your daily life. For example, this could mean going out of your way to watch television programs and movies about people who are from groups that might be less familiar to you, or that depict people in roles that don't fit with societal biases or stereotypes. In addition, you can work to learn more about systemic barriers that can serve to perpetuate stereotypes, biases, and inequalities in our society.
>
> An additional strategy involves changing the way that you make decisions. As a first step, it is worth reflecting on the fact that we hold biases that can influence the way we process information and how we make decisions. Instead of getting rid of these biases, we can try to make sure that they have less influence on our decisions.
>
> For example, when making hiring decisions, you might want to blind yourself to certain types of information about candidates… Another, potentially useful, strategy can include committing to decision criteria in advance. This can help eliminate the tendency to select candidates based on gut feelings (which can be based on stereotypes about who would "fit" the role the best) and then shift the criteria to match the qualifications of that candidate… In addition, collecting and assessing information in systematic ways can help ensure that you don't simply go with the person that immediately comes to mind.
>
> (https://implicit.harvard.edu/implicit/faqs.html, accessed 2024)

In the world of education, nameless grading might be a step toward combating bias and an opportunity to discover potential bias in our own grading. The use of a detailed rubric also can better prevent us from making judgments based on bias.

Uncovering implicit biases and recognizing these as a possible cause for avoidance of an individual can allow us to make changes to our otherwise natural behaviors. We can be more intentional in our actions and allow space for a relationship to be built that may never have been able to form in the distance created by our biases. These choices can even potentially rewire our brains to make positive rather than negative associations with the group from which that person identifies.

Devine, Forscher, Austin, and Cox (2012) similarly found strategies to be effective in reducing implicit racial bias for at least eight weeks. Approaching implicit bias as a habit to be broken, they developed a 12-week intervention that incorporated stereotype replacement, counter-stereotypic imaging, individuation, perspective-taking, and increased opportunities for contact. As they note, education and training both play important roles, and "several components likely work in combination to prompt situational awareness of one's bias and translate that awareness into chronic awareness, concern, and self-regulatory effort" (p. 1277).

In short, this is not easy work, but it is possible and is important in improving our relationships and ensuring alignment of our conscious and unconscious views. We believe that the actual effort – the time and mental energy – required to uncover and reflect upon biases has deterred many from embracing ABAR (anti-bias, anti-racist) practices. We also believe that much of this refusal stems from a person's own insecurities and unwillingness to face discomfort. It is not easy to learn unlovely things about ourselves, but this discomfort is the path to becoming better educators and people.

It is important to remember that the purpose of intentionally calling attention to what some might view as "flaws" in oneself is honorable. Temporary discomfort can ultimately lead to comfort, for us and those around us, in all our social interactions. If we can begin to do this for ourselves in a nonjudgmental way and recognize that awareness of our mistakes is both useful and necessary, we can prevent the stress-induced nervous system response and instead create moments of growth for ourselves and our students.

Addressing Bias in School Systems

Beyond addressing our own views, recognition of bias in educational institutions and curricular materials is crucial in making any headway toward dismantling them. The favoritism for narratives and histories that match that of able-bodied heterosexual cisgender white Christians in any curriculum should not only be examined by those teaching the curricula but also discussed with the students. As Justice (2023) reminds us, "The very existence of Black History Month is evidence of the centering of whiteness as everyday, normalized experience, as well as the ongoing struggle to resist it" (p. 171).

Ighodaro and Wiggan (2013) use the fitting term "curriculum violence" to describe the "deliberate manipulation of education and academic programs in a manner that marginalizes students and their learning experiences, as well as the intellectual and social-psychological well-being of omitted groups; signaling to learners that these groups have no contributions or are not worthy of inclusion" (p. 24). While some educators may suggest that following an established curriculum may not be a "deliberate" choice to omit the contributions of a particular cultural group, educators are (unfortunately) responsible for supplementing an inadequate curriculum if we want to prevent harm in our classrooms.

It is likely difficult to build feelings of trust and security with all students if we are ignoring, whether intentionally or unintentionally, the histories and lived experiences of our (greater) student population. Our individual teaching choices communicate biases regardless of the curriculum we are mandated to teach. While the ideal here would be an already-established inclusive curriculum, the reality is that this is not always the case, especially in a nation where misguided laws are continuing to limit the teaching of the valuable histories of members of our communities. At the very least, an expressed recognition of the inadequacy of a curriculum that omits the histories of marginalized groups – recognition of the curriculum bias – can help to validate students' feelings of invisibility. We can (and should) always ask "Who is missing?" and "Why is this important?" Beyond curriculum, students should be encouraged to ask these questions in other settings – social groups, community organizations, the media they consume – to cultivate habits of awareness and inclusion.

Further trends in the educational system – the disproportionately high enrollment of white and Asian American students in advanced courses or the disproportionately high numbers of Black and Latino student expulsion for example – and the structural reasons that these occur must also be acknowledged if we are to effectively confront bias on a larger scale (Groeger, Waldman, & Eads, 2018). We need to examine the contributing factors to such trends and the extent to which these patterns occur in our own communities and districts. Without this thorough examination, it may leave a person to assume that these trends occur because of inherent differences in the particular group rather than circumstances experienced by that group. This is a large reason why oppression can continue to exist, because the beliefs that hold up prejudice and discrimination have not been thoroughly examined and discredited. Intentional efforts can be made by school districts and governmental bodies to address such issues but, unfortunately, all too often, avoidance prevails.

Biases ultimately are the foundation for oppression. While we may not be able to remove or prevent the potential for oppression entirely from the institution of education, we can start with ourselves and the choices we make. Garrison (1996) offers, "The particular prejudices that we hold (or hold us) at a given moment determine our horizon. It is the limit not only of the actual but of the possibilities we can imagine" (p. 438). It is our responsibility as humans and educators to keep our eyes open for an ever-expanding horizon.

As educators we need to ensure that our biases do not affect our student-teacher interactions, our grading, our feedback, our discipline policies, and daily practices. These biases can be felt by others, even if they cannot be recognized by ourselves, and have the potential to increase the stress of students in a way that can negatively impact their learning and sense of belonging in a classroom. And the process of confronting these biases can free us of their limitations, making us more available to build relationships and community. Once we have set ourselves on an anti-bias path, we need to face the likelihood of related stress, which we explore in the next chapter.

Reflective Activities

- Ask yourself the following questions:
    - Have students ever accused you of demonstrating favoritism? How did you react?

    _____
    _____

    - Was there anything different you might change about your actions or response?

    _____
    _____

- Consider the identity groups of the students with whom you have the best student-teacher relationships. Are any groups overrepresented? If yes, why do you think this is?

    _____
    _____
    _____

- Identify specific things you do to build connections **with** students with whom you do not share identity groups or obvious interests.

    _____
    _____
    _____

- Identify specific things you do to build connections **among** students who may not share identity groups or obvious interests.

    _____
    _____
    _____

- Take an implicit association test (https://implicit.harvard.edu/implicit/takeatest.html) and debrief the results with an accountability partner. If you are uncomfortable with the results, set goals for yourself to rework your associations based on their suggestions.
- Take an inventory of the curriculum or programming you facilitate in your role as an educator. Who is missing? Why is this important?

    _____
    _____
    _____

References

Banaji, M. R., & Greenwald, A. G. (2016). *Blindspot: Hidden biases of good people*. New York: Bantam Books.

Barber, C., & Torney-Purta, J. (2008). The relation of high-achieving adolescents' social perceptions and motivation to teachers' nominations for advanced programs. *Journal of Advanced Academics, 19*, 412–443. https://doi.org/10.4219/jaa-2008-813

Bertrand, M., & Mullainathan, S. (2003). *Are Emily and Greg more employable than Lakisha and Jamal? A field experiment on labor market discrimination.*, NBER Working Paper No. 9873, Cambridge, MA: National Bureau of Economic Research.

Cotton, J., O'Neill, B., & Griffin, A. (2008). The 'Name Game': Affective and hiring reactions to first names. *Management Faculty Research and Publication, 3*. https://epublications.marquette.edu/mgmt_fac/3

DeSteno, D. (2015). *The truth about trust: How it determines success in life, love, learning, and more*. New York: Plume.

Devine, P. G., Forscher, P. S., Austin, A. J., & Cox, W. T. L. (2012). Long-term reduction in implicit race bias: A prejudice habit-breaking intervention. *Journal of Experimental Social Psychology, 48*(6), 1267–1278.

Elhoweris, H., Mutua, K., Alsheikh, N., & Holloway, P. (2005). Effect of children's ethnicity on teachers' referral and recommendation decisions in gifted and talented programs. *Remedial and Special Education, 26*(1), 25–31.

Garrison, J. (1996). A Deweyan theory of democratic listening. *Educational Theory, 46*, 429–451. https://doi.org/10.1111/j.1741-5446.1996.00429.x

Groeger, L., Waldman, A., & Eads, D.. (2018). *Miseducation: Is there racial inequality at your school?* ProPublica. https://projects.propublica.org/miseducation/

Ighodaro, E., & Wiggan, G. A. (2013). *Curriculum violence : America's new civil rights issue*. New York: Nova Science.

Justice, B. (2023). Schooling as a white good. *History of Education Quarterly, 63*(2), 154–178. https://doi.org/10.1017/heq.2023.7.

Kline, P., Rose, E. K., & Walters, C. R. (2022). Systemic discrimination among large U.S. Employers. *The Quarterly Journal of Economics, 137*(4), 1963–2036.

Marcus, G. (2008). *Kluge: The haphazard construction of the human mind*. New York: Houghton Mifflin.

McCloskey, J. (2020). *When truth is all you have: A memoir of faith, justice, and freedom for the wrongly convicted*. New York: Anchor Books.

Miner, H. (1956). Body ritual among the Nacirema. *American Anthropologist, 58*(3), 503–507. American Anthropological Association.

Project Implicit. (2011). *Project implicit: Frequently asked questions*. Harvard. https://implicit.harvard.edu/implicit/faqs.html.

Woodson, J., & López, R. (2018). *The day you begin*. New York: Nancy Paulsen Books.

9

Recognizing and Minimizing Stress

How to Identify Stressors and Practice Stress-Management Techniques to Benefit Ourselves and Our Students

Educating children is stressful. Just *interacting* with children can be stressful. We know. Thus far in the book we have suggested taking steps that require being vulnerable and deeply self-reflective. Having walked through this very process, we recognize that the act of doing this work may temporarily add to one's current feelings of stress. In fact, it really is to be expected. Becoming comfortable with the discomfort, while cliché, is exactly what a person has to experience for neuroplasticity to do its work.

It is natural to not want to invite *more* stress into our busy educator lives. This is likely the reason that we put off goals like confronting our own biases during the school year. Because we can relate to this feeling, we recognize the importance of developing strategies to handle negative stress, for ourselves and for our students. The hope is that when we are regularly and reliably able to decrease our stress levels, we are able to practice and maintain true self-care.

Kate's teaching responsibilities increased significantly this year, causing her a substantial amount of sustained work-related stress.

KMH: I have learned to do all the things: a healthy sleep routine – a reliable eight hours, meditation, mindfulness, yoga, exercise, stress management, cognitive behavioral therapy, leaning on loving friends, and all the rest of the family obligations – daughter to a mother with dementia, mother to two children, etc. I am doing all the things, but it's still not enough to lessen the daily sources of stress. With a candle burning and my first cup of coffee in my favorite mug, I need to start my day. But I have been awake since 3 AM because I woke up with heartburn again. The reason is stress because it wasn't anything I ate last night.

I am feeling a lot of teacher stress. And the greatest source of stress for me in teaching is knowing what I *could* have accomplished had I had the time. There is always more I could have done. Living with the missed chances and opportunities - not because I didn't want to, but because I couldn't due to the limitations of my time - is an ever-present source of psychological stress that never leaves me. This comes down to the ratio of me to the people assigned to my care each year.

Here are some of the things I was able to do more readily when I had only four class sections of 24 students each (under 100 students per year):

- I called parents during the day and talked with many of them and was able to help their children succeed. I still make these calls, but they are less frequent.
- I would walk once a week with a colleague and get exercise and stress relief while discussing work.
- I would create new teaching materials.
- I would regularly visit students during their study halls and work with them when they needed it.
- I would observe colleagues' lessons to learn new strategies, offer unofficial feedback if they asked, and discuss interdisciplinary connections.

I still do all these things. However, it's now a very tight squeeze from all directions. Now there is less overall time to plan, very little time to meet with colleagues, and much less time to grade. There is zero time to ever take a walk or have a chat with a colleague about teaching. There is simply so little free time left that I find myself, in one year's time, back in the survival mode of a new teacher. All other things being equal, these five sections of science energetically tap me out and take away the "extras" I was able to enjoy in an earlier part of my career. From an objective point of view, it is very useful to be able to share the contrast between teaching 96 people and 120 people.

My stress comes down to a constant fight for time. I also have little time to read science journals or education journals. Everything and anything, including the writing of this book, must be crammed into early mornings, weekends, and summer.

Identifying Stressors

The effects of psychological stress on a human's body and brain are pretty well-documented these days. While the following list is incomplete, teachers will likely experience any and all of these stress-related impacts on their health:

- Hypertension – sustained high blood pressure – is caused by the vasoconstriction of blood vessels when we are under stress. This puts strain on our hearts and is very difficult to detect or control without medical intervention, which is why hypertension is known as the "silent killer."
- Psychological stress results in muscle tension and pain.
- The cortisol release caused by stress throws hormones out of balance and causes a cascade effect which can make a person insulin-resistant and potentially lead to diabetes and obesity.
- We can actually get sick from stress as our immune system becomes compromised.
- Our bones break down when we experience a high mental stress load. The stress hormones slow bone growth and healing.
- The hippocampal cells of the brain are particularly sensitive to psychological stress and the presence of fight-or-flight hormones prevents the ability of the brain to function optimally and learn.
- We don't sleep as well, which prevents our brains from clearing out all the amyloid-beta and other metabolic waste products from daily brain cell functioning.

In short, teaching-related stress has the potential to ruin our bodies and brains. It is well-known that stress causes an array of inflammatory diseases – everything from diabetes and obesity to heart disease and dementia. These are huge concerns for teachers. We need our bodies and our brains. So, we need to be on high alert and we need to know how to manage the emotional toll of education-related professions.

We will all feel stress throughout our careers in education. It is unavoidable, as our work is *life* work. Unless we foster self-awareness to be able to recognize when we feel stress, our health and our relationships can suffer. We cannot overemphasize the importance of recognizing and addressing this stress in whatever way feels appropriate for you. With that said, we know that managing stress is the work of a lifetime for every human. For educators in particular, finding the balance and preempting unhealthy stress-relieving behavior is necessary to function optimally.

We can also utilize the "power of the pause" and reflection to help identify stressors that we may not have noticed before. For example, in conversation, are there certain topics that make us stumble over our words or increase the number of times we say "um"? Why is this? Bonilla-Silva (2022), in his research on race, has observed rhetorical incoherence – grammatical mistakes, lengthy pauses, and repetition – when people discuss sensitive topics such as race. In his research, he found that "almost all the [white] college students were incoherent when discussing certain racial issues, particularly their personal relationships with Blacks" (p. 120).

The stress related to topics that make us uncomfortable becomes obvious. Even if we want to hide discomfort, often our bodies will do the talking for us. Because of this, it is in everyone's best interest to understand the causes of such discomfort and to face it to prevent these occurrences from continuing.

Strategies to Minimize Educator Stress

While for some of us with severe trauma outside help may be required to heal, others may be able to improve their health outcomes and social interactions through intentional activities to care for our bodies and brains.

VK: I always laughed when administrators and other non-teachers reminded me to "take time for self-care" throughout my teaching career. I laughed because it was usually coupled with examples that seemed impossible like "get a massage" for a woefully underpaid teacher or "leave your grading at home" for a teacher who has actual grading deadlines. The reality is that finding adequate time to take care of oneself, while feeling the pressure of caring for so many young people (many times including our own young people at home), is often very difficult for educators. Yet, I have now become one of the people advocating for it, as I now realize that my lack of dedicated "self-care" time contributed to my position becoming entirely unsustainable.

It sounds wild now to think that my version of self-care - relieving myself of additional work - meant sometimes going to work even when I felt sick, so I didn't have to plan additional lessons and then grade the assignments and then also address the students who had chosen *not* to complete the assignment in my absence.

While I never really managed to effectively prioritize my own well-being during my full-time teaching career, the ways in which I relieved the stresses of work were through my interactions with my fellow colleagues, a number of whom have become some of my very best friends. Venting sessions were a must. Just knowing that others could relate to the immense stresses that a teacher faces daily made me feel better about whatever I was facing that day. On occasion, and only later in my career, I consciously chose to set aside grading and then always shared with the students that I had done so for a meaningful reason.

Self-care opportunities, rather than suggested by email, should be built into the profession and genuinely encouraged by administrators. Promoting self-care might be allowing for professional days for grading, working with teachers to develop realistic expectations for student work in the case of absences, decreasing class size, hiring additional staff to take over teacher duties that do not benefit their teaching, establishing a teacher-buddy system to allow for teachers to "tap out" if necessary, having private spaces for teachers to unwind and maybe even nap on a period off, creating a comfortable space and schedule for breastfeeding parents to pump, or developing an effective teacher-mentor system designed to assist new or struggling teachers. Ultimately, healthy teachers are better teachers, so these would be resources well spent.

We can encourage ourselves and one another to continue these intentional self-care opportunities outside of the work day. In Kate's case, writing serves as one way to handle the stresses of work. Years ago, Kate began allowing herself a "Kate Day," a few hours after work when she headed to the library instead of home. On "Kate Day" emails go unanswered, student work ungraded, and lessons unadjusted. She leaves her daily grind for a few hours to indulge in the joy of writing.

In Val's case, gardening is an important stress-relieving activity, especially now that she lives in a tropical paradise. Although she does not designate a "Val day," she frequents plant nurseries weekly and tries her best not to make too many purchases. As we have already mentioned, stress-relieving activities must be unique to one's personality. The relief of stress cannot be stressful. It must come naturally from the individual and mesh with their life as it is.

At the very basic level, we need to recognize healthy everyday activities to lower our stress levels. Burke Harris (2018) in *The Deepest Well* discusses the health impacts on individuals who have experienced high levels of stress due to adverse childhood experiences (ACEs). To combat these, she suggests regular exercise, ensuring good sleep hygiene, and engaging in mindfulness practices in order to reduce stress hormones, reduce inflammation, enhance neuroplasticity, and help our immune system to function effectively.

Kate has been practicing mindfulness, meditation, and yoga for 20 years.

KMH: At an art retreat in Maine in 2008, my fifth-grade art teacher asked me if I ever used the "moment of silence" technique in my classes, and I told her I didn't. I suddenly realized that I had never even thought to transfer this mindfulness practice to my own teaching. Every class of my childhood school had begun with the teacher saying, "Let's begin with a moment of silence." It was always quick, maybe 30 seconds. Each teacher did it differently. No one ever forgot to do it, though, in my recollection, it blended with all the many other memories.

In the fall of 2008, I returned to my classroom and implemented my first version of mindfulness in the classroom, what I called "Sixty Seconds of Silence." I would say and still do, "Let's bring peace to our bodies and our brains." During this time, I would ask the students to sit quietly without moving or speaking. I never told them to close their eyes, nor did I teach them breathwork. That would come in the years that followed. Now, we call it "The Peace," and we "anchor down" together. The time is variable and I usually say a meaningful quote that aligns with our guiding question of the day. In short, in seeking my own meaningful ways to find peace and manage stress, I have created a stress-management routine I can share every hour in my classes. This has served to keep me calm and emotionally regulated and does the same for my students. It has been a life-improving intervention and it continues to evolve.

Identifying and Addressing Student Stressors

Educators are in the unique position of needing to recognize and address their own stress as well as the stress of the students in their care. While this may be possible to do when we see students behaving differently or acting out, providing opportunities to gain insight into the lives of students can also be a helpful way to assist them in identifying their own stressors and addressing them in healthy ways.

As we have referenced throughout the book, modeling and discussing our own stress-reducing methods can serve as meaningful opportunities to teach. It offers possibilities, allowing students to observe how another person operates and then choose a method that works with their individual personalities. Even if a student chooses not to do a single thing offered by the teacher, at least they now understand that this is an important part of being human and can seek out what resonates personally with them. For example, many of our students may utilize video games for stress reduction; while this is completely valid, it may not be a method we model.

At a basic level, helping students to name stress where it occurs in their lives can be empowering. They may experience physical reactions associated with stress but may never have understood those reactions to be related to specific stressors. As a yearly lesson in Val's elective course, she asked students to name sources of stress in their lives, identify the impacts, and consider ways in which teachers and administrators could alleviate some of these stresses.

VK: The top causes of stress (pre-pandemic) were consistent: heavy school workload, balancing school/work/extracurricular activities, teacher miscommunication, navigating future plans (college applications and decisions primarily), social expectations, the late and absence policies, and the general loss of control within the school.

The last cause was always the most interesting for me as it was expressed in a variety of ways and usually with the most anger. Students would share specific stories about administration or other teachers restricting their freedoms (ex. not allowing them to leave the room as needed) or accusing them of misbehavior. They would say that school felt "like a prison" with the monitoring of all student movement throughout the building. They resented their perceived inability to complete basic tasks for comfort when they wanted (stand up and stretch, use the bathroom, eat food, respond to their mom's text) and interpreted this as a "lack of trust." Interestingly, this loss of control is cited as a top stressor for teachers as well in many educational settings. For example, having to hold one's bladder for hours at a time, especially while pregnant, can be a real challenge.

Teacher miscommunication also showed up on our lists in various ways, but one of the most meaningful and consistent comments was about teachers "not understanding" or not relating to students and their backgrounds. While I recognize the lengths to which teachers go to ensure adequate communication in verbal and written ways, I also recognize that much of this "communication" with students is non-verbal and likely unconscious. I felt compelled to research this further once I began to see the trends in student data, and I began to look for, and work with teachers to uncover, ways to prevent these forms of "miscommunication." While there are many types of miscommunication, those that result in student stress and the inability to connect with teachers and learn most effectively have the greatest impact on the student-teacher relationship.

As discussed in previous chapters, understanding the true causes of our behaviors can help us to address and change those that result in negative outcomes for ourselves and our students. As much as we do not like to face it, we all have biases that surface in our interactions with others. These biases directly impact our behaviors and consequently how others *feel* in our presence. How can a student, or anyone for that matter, focus fully on a task or feel like a member of a supportive community if they feel judged or misunderstood? These microaggressions, defined as negative "subtle, stunning, often automatic, and nonverbal exchanges" that function as insults, can effectively destroy a student-teacher relationship and sabotage attempts to build community (Pierce, Carew, Pierce-Gonzalez, & Wills, 1977). Our facial responses alone – tension in the brow, movement of the lip, slight tilt of the head – signal our emotions, positive and negative, to others (Ekman, 2007). Obviously, any experience that signals negativity or distance from a teacher will cause damage to a relationship with a student, just as it would if we had these experiences with any adult.

Regardless of the intent of a microaggression, the resulting stress response is automatic and therefore cannot be avoided. It would not matter if the teacher did not *intend* to make the student feel this way or if they said things like "I treat everyone the same" or "I don't see color." In fact, these comments then serve to reaffirm the hurtful action since the person is unwilling to decenter themselves and take accountability. Beyond the immediate stress and impact in the classroom, continued microaggressions have been found to have significant health impacts on targeted populations due to the associated automatic stress response (Chae et al., 2014; Sue, Capodilupo, & Holder, 2008). Even the *fear* of being stereotyped, known as stereotype threat, has been shown to have negative impacts in the classroom (Steele, 2010). While it can be difficult to acknowledge and face our own biases, we cannot effectively serve our students if we cannot be willing to do this.

Strategies to Address Stress Related to Bias

Professional development related to bias is sorely needed. Of course, teachers can individually take steps to research implicit bias, as we have previously discussed, and learn more about the histories of groups with which they are the most unfamiliar. However, school districts need to make more opportunities available to allow teachers the time and space to reflect together. They may also take steps to make the profession of teaching manageable enough to allow teachers to take on the mental load of tackling bias. For something this emotionally difficult to address, strategic scaffolded guidance is most effective. Further, teacher preparation programs need to emphasize racial literacy, the skills to "read, recast, and resolve racially stressful encounters," so that teachers are equipped before entering the field (Stevenson, 2014, p. 62).

The best professional development workshop Val has attended was one run by the Racial Empowerment Collaborative and the Lion's Story that focused on building racial literacy and decreasing racial stress. She sought out this opportunity based on the suggestion of an amazing former student and her inspiring older sister, and the district reimbursed for her attendance. Howard Stevenson, who led the seminar, defines racial socialization as "the transmission and acquisition of intellectual, emotional, and behavioral skills to protect and affirm racial self-efficacy by recasting and reducing the stress that occurs during racial conflicts with the goal of successfully resolving these conflicts" (Stevenson, 2014, p. 18). There is a lot packed into that definition, and all of it is necessary. Educators need to increase their racial socialization skills, not only for the students but also to better themselves – their health and relationships – and ultimately our communities.

Educators often avoid engaging in conversations about race, religion, sexuality, and gender due to the discomfort caused by it. Now, the laws of some states even aim to prevent these discussions. Fears of provoking conflict and "saying the wrong thing," likely due to inadequate understanding of the topic, have contributed to the lack of discussion of important political and societal topics. This results in feelings of invisibility and isolation for many of our students, further adding to their stress (Page, 2017; Solórzano, Ceja, & Yosso, 2000). Learning the skills to effectively navigate the stress response during uncomfortable conversations can allow for these discussions to occur. Such discussions are necessary in education to promote equity, feelings of comfort and safety, and to help students to become more aware and productive citizens. The stifling of such conversations, as may now be the case in a number of states passing anti-education laws, results in negative societal impacts, contributing to further political polarization and the inability of citizens to come to a place of understanding and compromise. We need to practice and then model the importance of acknowledging and confronting, rather than ignoring, topics such as racism and oppression, to benefit our students but also to better our local and national communities.

When educators and pre-service teachers understand the negative impacts of stress in the classroom, we can work strategically to provide a truly safe and healthy learning environment. So, how can we best provide a supportive classroom that aims to reduce student stress based on identity group? We have listed below some starting suggestions based on our conversations with students.

- ◆ Learn, acknowledge, and discuss the legacy of societal privileges for cisgender, heterosexual, able-bodied, Christian, white American citizens, and the legacies of discrimination and segregation.

- Specify exactly which people are referenced when textbooks and classroom materials, particularly history books, refer to general groups.
- Emphasize the value of learning from diverse perspectives, including those of students.
- Welcome, solicit, and utilize student feedback.
- Listen to and validate student experiences of micro- and macroaggressions.
- Reflect on our own words, actions, and behaviors (conscious and unconscious) and their impact on students.
- Allow students to self-identify race or gender (when appropriate) rather than assuming.
- Avoid assuming that everyone will experience something in the same way we do.
- Avoid singling out students for their perspective as a member of an identity group.
- Research the use of coded language as descriptors for a group (e.g., "ghetto," "thugs," "urban," "ethnic," "bossy") and avoid using these words.
- Know the dates of religious and cultural holidays and be mindful of these when assigning due dates.
- Invite conversation and understanding, rather than becoming defensive, when faced with suggestions of prejudice or racism.
- Recognize that a person's intentions make little difference to the target of a micro- or macroaggression.
- Reject a "colorblind" philosophy as it dismisses a person's racial experiences and history and can be interpreted as blind to racism.
- Preview course content that may be particularly upsetting for certain identity groups, especially content that may depict violence or slurs.

Stress from past traumas remains with us – "As long as the trauma is not resolved, the stress hormones that the body secretes to protect itself keep circulating, and the defensive movements and emotional responses keep getting replayed" (van der Kolk, 2014, p. 66). This applies to students who have experienced trauma as well as educators. While we may not be in a space to help students resolve their traumas, we can create an emotionally safe classroom where students feel supported and valued. In fact, serving as a trusted, safe, dependable adult for students can alone serve as a way to help them heal (Perry, 2006/2017). Our own traumas, however, should not only be addressed to benefit our physical health but also our ability to best serve in our capacities as educators.

In sum, seeking to identify and address stressors in our own personal and professional lives serves to benefit our health, our relationships, and our teaching practice. We can then be in a better place to help students to address stressors of their own and, importantly, any that *we* may exacerbate. As Jensen (2015) reminds us, not only is stress "terrible for learning," but "the effect of stressful experiences and emotional trauma on adolescents can have serious consequences for mental and emotional health later in life" (p. 131). Recognizing and minimizing stress then becomes paramount to the creation of classrooms in which students can feel safe and balanced enough to utilize their energy for meaningful learning.

Reflective Activities

- Identify your biggest cause of stress at work.
    - What is one step that you could take to lessen this stress?

    _____
    _____
    _____
    _____
    _____

    - What is one step administration could take to lessen this stress?

    _____
    _____
    _____
    _____

    - *Bonus activity: Share this with your administrators if you feel comfortable!*
- Identify what self-care looks like for you. How can you prioritize this more effectively?

    _____
    _____
    _____
    _____

- Rate your comfort levels (1–10) when talking about race-related topics with…
    - adults of the same perceived racial background _____
    - adults of a different perceived racial background _____
    - students of the same perceived racial background _____
    - students of a different perceived racial background _____
- After completing the activity above, consider the following questions:
    - Are there differences in comfort level when talking with people of the same race as compared to people of different races? If yes, why? Why might this be problematic?

    _____
    _____
    _____
    _____

- Are there differences in comfort levels when talking with students as compared to adults? If yes, why? Why might this be problematic?

  _____
  _____
  _____
  _____

- Would these same comfort level differences apply to individuals of different religious, cultural, gender, or sexuality groups? Why/why not?

  _____
  _____
  _____
  _____

References

Bonilla-Silva, E. (2022). *Racism without racists: Color-blind racism and the persistence of racial inequality in America*. Sixth edition. Lanham, MD: Rowman and Littlefield.

Burke Harris, N. (2018). *The deepest well: Healing the long-term effects of childhood adversity*. New York: Houghton Mifflin Harcourt.

Chae, D. H., Nuru-Jeter, A. M., Adler, N. E., Brody, G. H., Lin, J., Blackburn, E. H., & Epel, E. S. (2014). Discrimination, racial bias, and telomere length in African-American men. *American Journal of Preventive Medicine, 46*(2), 103–111. https://doi.org/10.1016/j.amepre.2013.10.020

Ekman, P. (2007). *Emotions revealed: Recognizing faces and feelings to improve communication and emotional life*. New York: Macmillan.

Jensen, F. (2015). *The teen brain: A neuroscientist's survival guide to raising adolescents and young adults*. New York: HarperCollins.

Page, M. L. (2017). Teaching in the cracks: Using familiar pedagogy to advance LGBTQ-inclusive curriculum. *Journal of Adolescent & Adult Literacy, 60*(6), 677–685. http://www.jstor.org/stable/26630689

Perry, B. (2006/2017). *The boy who was raised as a dog and other stories from a child psychiatrist's notebook: What traumatized children can teach us about loss, love, and healing*. New York: Basic Books.

Pierce, C. M., Carew, J. V., Pierce-Gonzalez, D., & Wills, D. (1977). An experiment in racism: TV commercials. *Education and Urban Society, 10*(1), 61–87. https://doi.org/10.1177/001312457701000105

Solórzano, D., Ceja, M., & Yosso, T. (2000). Critical race theory, racial microaggressions, and campus racial climate: The experiences of African American college students. *The Journal of Negro Education, 69*(1/2), 60–73. http://www.jstor.org/stable/2696265

Steele, C. (2010). *Whistling Vivaldi: How stereotypes affect us and what we can do*. New York: W.W. Norton & Company.

Stevenson, H. C. (2014). *Promoting racial literacy in schools: Differences that make a difference*. New York: Teachers College Press.

Sue, D. W., Capodilupo, C. M., & Holder, A. M. B. (2008). Racial microaggressions in the life experience of Black Americans. *Professional Psychology: Research and Practice, 39*(3), 329–336.

van der Kolk, B. A. (2015). *The body keeps the score: Brain, mind, and body in the healing of trauma*. New York: Penguin Books.

10

Increasing Educator Flexibility

How to Release Traditional Teacher Control to Strengthen Student-Teacher Connection

Lesson planning and structure are obviously essential to a well-functioning classroom, but real-life experiences can and will serve as interruptions throughout one's teaching career, really throughout one's day. How a teacher manages these interruptions results in either a building up or a deterioration of the student-teacher relationship and/or a student's learning, depending on the occurrence. According to the Danielson (2013) evaluation rubric, a "distinguished" teacher "seizes an opportunity to enhance learning, building on a spontaneous event or students' interests, or successfully adjusts and differentiates instruction to address individual student misunderstandings" (p. 83). Heavers (2012) refers to some of these types of learning opportunities as "telling breaks" and recognizes that "teachers who open themselves up to possibilities that the telling break can render will be better able to integrate the symbolic universe of the school with the real life experiences of those it is designed to educate" (p. iv).

These are the moments in which a teacher's authentic self is revealed, or rather, whether they display willingness to let their authentic self show. These are the moments that students remember years later. These are the moments when the most meaningful learning occurs.

The Importance of Educator Flexibility

Flexibility is yet another important life skill that educators should model for students, as we all know that the interruption of plans *is* life. By naming what we are doing, we are helping students to explicitly see how one can recognize that something unexpected has occurred and how to navigate the disruption effectively. So rather than panicking at interruptions, which we might be inclined to do, especially during our early teaching years or during observations, we might want to reframe these moments and value them for the learning opportunities that they are.

Additionally, flexibility applies to our relationships with our students and our treatment of them. As Noddings (2013) explains, "Variation is to be expected if the one claiming to care really cares, for her engrossment is in the variable and never fully understood other, in the particular other, in a particular set of circumstances" (p. 24). Showing students that we truly care about them and want the best for them requires treating them as they need to be treated. This effectively means that we will not necessarily be treating students equally; rather, we will be treating them equitably. For example, if a student experiences the loss of a family member, the flexible (and appropriate) response by the teacher would be to adjust due dates to accommodate the student's situation. Maintaining rigidity – even if it is for a noble reason like ensuring equality for students – can rupture relationships if we are unable to *see* a student and their needs in a time of uncertainty.

KMH: "When you come to the door of your classroom, Katie," my kindergarten teacher once told me, "hold your hand on the handle and pause for a moment. Prepare to allow whatever happens to happen."

I can only speak for myself, but it keeps my anxiety low when I have a very specific plan for a lesson I'm teaching and I'm able to know in advance pretty much how it will run. It's just a nice feeling of confidence, competence, and comfort all balled up into that lovely feeling of a tightly planned lesson you feel good about: it's aligned with the standards, has a nice balance of skill and knowledge that the students will learn, and will roll out without trouble or fuss.

The thing about this theoretical experience I've described above is that a lesson rarely ever rolls out as we plan. Instead, a thousand possible variables crop up to change how the learning experiences unfold, and these are rarely predictable. The only certainty in teaching is that something will occur that we could never have imagined, and we are going to have to roll with it. This degree of flexibility has been something that has simply happened to me over the years. I didn't purposefully set out to have a more flexible brain in the classroom; I simply had to in order to survive. This has, over the two and a half decades I've taught, turned me into someone who embraces spontaneity and plans much more loosely than I ever imagined I would when I first stepped into the profession.

A few examples come to mind: changing the grouping, changing questions on the spot, or dropping a plan entirely and doing something completely different as suggested by a student. There are umpteen ways that I have abandoned a plan in favor of a different approach, and it's almost always at the suggestion of the students. They always seem to learn, over the course of the year, that I am open and interested in their feedback mid-lesson, and so it's no big deal at all to do an about-face and take a different tack.

We know there is no *one* way to teach something, just like there is no *one* way to do any specific thing. We embrace allowing students to think of ways that are better for them to learn or complete a particular task. This empowers them and makes their voices front and center in the learning process. We provide the "suggested" learning map (the carefully planned, standards-aligned lesson) and they run with it.

Flexibility in Responsiveness to Students

Flexibility then isn't just about the planning; it moves far beyond what we generally know as differentiation. Certainly, highly effective teaching requires daily differentiation of a lesson plan. Here, we suggest embracing a deeper degree of emotional and intellectual flexibility than is typically associated with the adaptations to a lesson plan based on learning levels. It means increasing the breadth and depth with which we can be responsive to the needs of the students and changing what we originally thought would work for them upon seeing where they *actually* are. Essentially, it is differentiating the differentiated material. It means adjusting, and it means meeting our students where they are. It means never letting ourselves be wedded to one particular way of thinking about or teaching something, because what works beautifully with one student might completely fail to serve another. Flexibility is a prerequisite for being willing and able to differentiate the differentiated at a higher level of emotional awareness.

Anyone who taught through the pandemic knows the importance of teacher flexibility. In a matter of days, or hours, teachers and administrators needed to transition to virtual learning, in part or in whole. This forced flexibility pushed many teachers (those who had the energy and care to do so) to rethink and reassess each lesson in the hopes of maximizing student learning during a time of turmoil. Educators needed to learn new technology and develop new assessment strategies overnight. The silver lining of this reevaluation of lesson plans and learning tools was that it permitted the experimentation that many teachers shed early in their careers after finding their go-to strategies. A great deal of useful reflection and high-quality teaching was born of the pandemic, despite the fact that many of the negative educational aspects have stuck in the public's memory. While these reflections would have been more welcome over a longer time frame, allowing for teachers to escape panic-mode teaching, the experience highlighted the importance of experimenting and adjusting teaching to be specific to the needs of the *specific* students in one's class during any given time. Plans and assessments from 20 years earlier, while potentially effective, need to be, at the very least, reconsidered to ensure that they meet the needs and promote the learning of the students in our classrooms.

Pandemic or not, teaching in a flexible way models risk-taking and experimentation for students. We believe that we should always be willing to do what we ask our students to do, and we encourage our students to take academic risks in an effort to grow. As leaders in the classroom, there is no better encouragement than to practice this ourselves.

In order to do this, we need to cultivate psychological flexibility, recognizing that this is an ideal to which we all must work toward.

KMH: I used to think that, after some unknown but finite number of years spent practicing the art of teaching, I would finally feel so comfortable that it would become relaxing and rather effortless: the learning would unfold beautifully and without interruption. I dreamed that the fruit of my many decades of hard work would be some harvest of ease. It's been no such thing. In fact, the longer I have spent in the classroom, the more I have begun to question the fundamental practices that seemed such a given, so solid, so definite.

Take, for example, all these needs:

- for everyone to be doing the same thing at the same time
- for everyone to hand their completed assignments in at the very same time
- for me to be the authority and best source of information for the students
- that everyone arrive on time during a very small and finite window, regardless of how far away their previous class is, or whether they needed to use the bathroom, or whether they were offering comfort or counsel to a friend in the hallway on the way to their next class

As my brain has become more flexible, I have become more discerning about my pedagogical choices. I am more intentional and less arbitrary: I don't make choices just because that is how I was taught, that is what my favorite teacher did, or this is what my colleagues do. Rather, I have been taught to continually experiment and I happily question *all* my choices in the classroom. The more I learn from Val, the more I learn not to take my teaching personally: we don't have to be our habits! Instead, we can be agents of continuous learning and therefore agents of great change.

Re-Envisioning Control in the Classroom

In order to allow ourselves the freedom to be flexible, we first need to break our preconceived notions about what effective instruction looks like. As discussed in a previous chapter, our biases permeate all aspects of our lives, including extending to what "good" or "effective" teaching looks like. The images that come to mind when we think of "good teaching" come from teachers we have had in the past, teachers we have observed, the media, our teacher preparation courses, and maybe our own prior teaching. It makes sense that we would want to emulate "effective teaching," but let us always consider whether we are doing so at our students' expense.

Does sitting comfortably in a place we feel is "effective" prevent us from experimenting to find new methods to further learning? And are these methods *truly* effective or do we just think they are? Are they effective for all students or only for some students? Just because we believe something to be "great teaching" does not mean that we should not also question it and get feedback from those we are serving – the students. While we want to continue practices proven by research to be effective, ultimately the best teaching is that which is responsive to our specific students.

Flexibility and a growth mindset are crucial here in order to break any bias. Just as we want students to question and grow, we need to do the same. And, in doing so, we will need to become more comfortable with releasing some of our control in the classroom.

Control in the classroom is a must, to keep the students safe, to keep a healthy routine, and an atmosphere of predictability and rational behavior. But we want to avoid teachers keeping all control over what happens in their classroom firmly in their own hands because this prevents students from practicing self-regulation and being active participants in their own learning. If we can get to the place where a modicum of control remains in the hands of the teacher – taking attendance, reporting grades, deciding the question of the day, stating the objective for the lesson, and so on – we allow the rest of the control to be in the hands of the students.

There are many ways Kate has worked to do this in the classroom. Her class nominates students who are interested in becoming class secretary and then, after speeches, they have a vote. This leader of the class becomes a liaison, a bridge between Kate and their classmates. There are different group leaders for activities and labs in every class. They use student-created or student-modified rubrics and peers grade one another for presentations and projects. The power she maintains is the grading of summative assessments and creating the plan for the week. Even then, as the year progresses, she allows for more and more student-devised learning experiences.

Kate has recognized that if an educator teaches her students how the decision-making process works – not the knee-jerk reaction or the reflex of just saying yes or no – the thoughtful step-by-step thinking process allows for contemplative choice-making. They no longer will have any need to exert day in and day out inexorable control of their students. She has made a daily practice of finding something she can hand over to her students: open the window if it feels stuffy; turn off some of the lights if you can't see the screen; go sneeze or drink water in the hallway. Don't ask, don't wait, just make the choice and do what you need to do. Val had the same policy with the students; she added the element of students' providing a thumbs up or thumbs down to indicate whether they needed her assistance in the hallway.

Since students have been trained to exist in classrooms where all the control and power is wielded by the teacher, it's a slow process to ask students to assume responsibility and control over their own choices, and more importantly and specifically, over their own learning. In the end, though, we should remind ourselves that we are human beings with an ancient limbic system (the reptilian brain) and a fear-causing amygdala. When we, as a collective whole, stop living in the fear of a loss of control, and instead live in shared control over our destiny, then there is the greatest potential for empowerment and learning.

We firmly believe that giving up control in the classroom will come more easily as educators increase their confidence and feelings of security in the classroom. In talking to a student teacher recently about how to balance health and workload, Val remembered one of the first times she passed over lesson responsibility to the students simply because she was too sick to lead the class. The students were tasked with locating a resource related to the lesson topic, reading it and developing a discussion question, and switching these resources with a partner to discuss afterward. It led to one of the lightbulb moments that we have as teachers when something finally clicks. This wasn't lazy teaching, this was *effective* teaching! Increasing student responsibility, especially when coupled with student choice, builds student skills and empowers them.

Passing over responsibility to the students obviously requires preparing them to meet these challenges. In the example above, teaching the skills of locating resources and developing effective discussion questions would be prerequisite skills needed to make this a truly effective lesson. However, creating structures to allow students to learn on their own terms can be one of the most powerful ways for students to learn. Creating space for this does require shedding the traditional notion of what teaching *should* look like, something that is often difficult to do early in our careers when we (likely) are most worried about not meeting expectations.

As Kate once said, "Ego matters. It holds you accountable. It makes you wash your hair." The problem is when an individual has too much ego, when they think they are *too* important or *more* important than the others in the room. An overactive ego, which generally indicates unhealed insecurity, can lead to a desire to control in a way that is limiting for others. We need to check our own egos and determine whether we feel discomfort allowing others to take over responsibilities in the classroom, and most importantly, *why* this discomfort occurs.

We need to remain free from the feeling that we are the keepers of knowledge and that we alone can lead the class. We need to practice humility in order to recognize what is truly best in the classroom even when it is not the way that we have been teaching for years. As already discussed, we all have blind spots and humility is required to address those in a meaningful way. Even in writing this chapter, we recognize that our teaching experiences are representative of the district in which we taught/teach, and that these suggestions may not fit with those in districts with different assets and needs. Our hope is that our experiences, even if not an exact match with your own, feel more relatable than non-educator perspectives and, at the least, allow you to reflect on your own choices in the classroom in a new way. We know that our teaching was not, and will not be, "perfect" and that is because we each have made conscious decisions to recognize and confront areas in which we can grow, even when it is painful to acknowledge.

These practices of control-checking are perhaps most important when we consider negative interactions we may have with students. These are the cases in which we likely have the greatest capacity for anger and defensiveness. Here we will discuss our perspectives regarding some of these difficult, and common, occurrences in the classroom and how we can recalibrate our brains and emotions to look at the situations more objectively.

One example might be when we think that a student doesn't like us. In this case, it may be helpful to think through the possible reasons that we have this perception. First, we can consider whether the behavior that has led us to think that the student doesn't like us is rooted in something else. We can try having a conversation with the student about those behaviors, rather than sharing "I think you don't like me" to find out. For example, we might offer,

"I notice that you roll your eyes in class when I am speaking." We might find out that they are masking their misunderstanding of the content or that they find our class boring or they just have problems with their contact lenses.

The conversation itself is key to opening our doors to them and being vulnerable, as it is a very human need to feel accepted by our own students. Otherwise, we may run the risk of them *actually*, and permanently, disliking us, which brings us to the second point. Students may not like us (yet) because of something we have actively done – an instance of miscommunication or an example of "not understanding" some aspects of their lives. Again, and even more importantly here, the conversation is needed and the focus needs to be on the harm done to the student, rather than our intention or guilt. This can provide us with the opportunity to apologize and repair the damage done or to agree with their anger at a certain policy that we are obligated to enforce. It is important for these conversations to occur privately, as the student may act differently with an audience. It also allows the opportunity to prepare ourselves for any feelings of defensiveness that might arise within us. We can role-play beforehand with a colleague or accountability partner if we anticipate high stress in the encounter and journal or debrief with someone we trust. We can always return to the conversation at another time if we need to exit to maintain calmness.

The bottom line is that these are our students, and they are still developing humans. They will have behaviors that annoy us, they will overreact, and they will be impulsive. They are also dealing with many emotions and likely many stressors about which we are unaware. We are there as adults to model the behaviors, social skills, and conflict resolution that they need to learn. By doing this effectively, we can also alleviate our own stress that we may feel upon entering a classroom where we know we will encounter a student from whom we feel negative energy.

Flexibility as It Relates to Discipline

For us, teacher flexibility extends to issues of discipline, as we believe that responses to student behaviors should be based on individual circumstances and need.

VK: During my student teaching, a colleague suggested that I remove a student from the room for "disrespectful behavior" when she refused to answer a seemingly simple question and put her head down. I felt very uncomfortable doing it, which is why I hadn't up until that point, but assumed that it was the right thing to do, as I was still learning best practices. Sending this student to administration felt both inauthentic and inappropriate, and I met with her as soon as I had the opportunity to discuss what happened. I found out that she didn't know the answer to my question and didn't want to "look stupid" in front of the class.

Once I realized that her "misbehavior" was essentially my fault, as I hadn't ensured that she understood the content basics or created an environment in which she felt comfortable admitting that, I realized that I needed to do better. I also decided that I would address similar behavioral issues moving forward privately without sending students to administration. Sending a student out felt like I was giving up on them and not making an effort to understand their motivation for the behavior. In doing so, I was losing the opportunity to build rapport and help them grow. A large part of my classroom management strategy was shaped by that one experience.

What does effective classroom management look like to you? If your answer is "compliance," consider why and the message that this sends to students. Compliance suggests that we, as teachers, are the ones in control and the ones that we want to remain in control. If we want to foster student responsibility and empowerment, we need to reframe this thinking to allow for students to have greater control in the classroom. In our experience, giving students greater control and responsibility has led to less disruption rather than more, as students have been more invested in their learning.

The goal is to have a classroom community established that functions in a way that prevents negative behaviors and that holds students accountable in a loving way when a breach of expectations occurs. Val has often heard from students that they were punished for something that they were not aware was disrespectful to a teacher. We should consider whether our classroom management model includes the explicit discussion of appropriate and inappropriate behaviors to ensure that there are no surprises for students. For example, if we have a preconceived idea of the time a bathroom trip should take, we might make that expectation clear to students and maybe even provide a reminder on the pass or sign-out sheet. These explicit discussions, and reminders of these discussions, help allow for clearer communication of expectations and also help to build skills for students, particularly those who may have difficulty reading social cues. Preemptively collecting information from students about how they prefer others to approach them in times of stress or crisis can also be helpful in responding most effectively to behavioral issues or personal crises that may occur during the year.

When a behavior does occur that is disruptive to one's learning or that of another, because it will no matter how hard we try to prevent it, our handling of it can impact our future relationship with that student and potentially their engagement level in school altogether. It can also impact the other students in the room, especially in cases in which the behavior impacts their feelings of safety. Traditional ways of meting out punishment, such as yelling at a student that we are serving them detention and continuing on with class, will be perceived as not honoring the dignity and growth of a student even though the aim is to hold them accountable. Instead, we should prioritize understanding the purpose of the misbehavior if we want to address it most effectively, maintain the relationship with the student, and prevent it from happening again.

Simply asking a student what happened seems so simple, yet is often not done. If a student is late to class, we believe that the "why" matters. If a student curses out their teacher, we believe the "why" matters. The personal affront may take practice to endure – *we know it's rough* – but it allows one to see beyond the surface. Addressing the "why" is how we build trust, rooted in caring, and ultimately help the student to grow. This has helped us to cultivate strong relationships with our habitually late students and has also helped us to realize how many "off-task" students were actually just confused and needed individual support. Knowing the motivation and the student's perspective of their own actions can also help guide us to provide choices of alternative behaviors for the student as a way to curb the behavior.

A traditional zero-tolerance discipline framework does not take circumstances, experiences, and prevention into account. Such zero-tolerance policies are often misused and flawed, and they do not directly address the root causes of misbehaviors (Martinez, 2009). Instead, to best meet students where they are, we favor policies that focus on learning, growth, and community. One of the most simple yet meaningful classroom management strategies is using affective statements and questions. It can serve as both a preventative and responsive measure and can help students to consider the impacts of their behaviors. Suggesting different activities for students engaging in disruptive behaviors, coupled with private conversations afterward, has also served as a successful strategy for addressing misbehaviors while maintaining the flow of the lesson. For example, when a student (we can call them Alex) was throwing objects across the room, an obvious attention-seeking behavior, Val would ask if they wanted to help click through the presentation, create a discussion question for the class, or draw a visual representation of the lesson content for the class. Of course, she would ask them to pick up the objects afterward, but she knew that maintaining their dignity in front of their peers was important. In this way, she allowed them to maintain a sense of control and make a positive choice to complete another attention-providing task.

There may also be cases in which a class discussion is necessary to restore the sense of community, like if a student was injured by Alex's projectiles. Kate's example below will discuss another instance of this. These discussions

– effectively, restorative circles – provide a supportive atmosphere in which students can discuss how the behavior made them feel and allow them to reflect in community. It is important to help students maintain focus on the behavior rather than the student, relating the behavior to something each student can identify with in their own lives, and to allow each student the opportunity to be heard. Ending the discussion by talking about positive ways to move forward is the most effective strategy and, again, helps students feel like they have control over the happenings in the classroom.

For more serious behavioral issues, the International Institute for Restorative Practices (IIRP) suggests using targeted questioning in more formal conference settings, with all parties impacted, to help the student(s) take accountability, prevent reoccurrence, and allow for reintegration and healing (Costello, Wachtel, & Wachtel, 2009/2019). In these cases, we should incorporate reflective activities that help students to identify the impact of their behaviors and to self-correct if the behavior resurfaces. Regardless of their age, students need to be taught skills for behavior in the same way that other skills are taught in the classroom.

How we address negative behaviors greatly impacts our connections with students and subsequently their engagement levels and feelings of empowerment. Addressing behaviors that make us angry also requires a lot of self-awareness and self-control to move forward in the most effective ways. We need to be aware when we have been triggered and notice our body's physical reactions. Ideally, we will have practiced appropriate responses in advance. This way, they can become automatic rather than a sudden outburst and hastily decided punishment. We also need to be aware of our own consistency in addressing misbehavior to be sure that we are not unconsciously targeting any group of students.

KMH: Once a student asked for a pass to the nurse and I wrote her one. About 45 minutes after she had been gone, I went into the attendance/grading program for some other reason and just had the thought to check and make sure she had arrived safely at the nurse. She was not entered in as having been to the nurse, so I called down. She had never arrived. I didn't get angry, but instead worried: What had happened to intercept her? A class effort began to locate her. I asked my class secretary to get on the phone with her and encourage her to come back to class. I called the vice principal and told him she was missing. I called the nurse again. I made sure that everyone knew I was searching for this child and that it was out of concern and *not* out of anger or ego. Because it wasn't.

After the class had been dismissed, the student arrived at my classroom door, and we talked it out. She told me she had left class to go sit with a friend who was hurting. In order to allow for full transparency with her, I made sure to explain that I had had to call the vice principal in the frenzy of trying to find her and that she might have to talk to him. We agreed together that a Saturday as punishment wouldn't be an appropriate consequence but that we should focus on building back our relationship and restrengthening our trust. And that was that.

The next day, since the whole class had been in on the search for her with me, I let everyone know that the student had been missing from class because she had gone to comfort a friend. I don't actually know for sure that this is what happened, but I decided to paint her in the most favorable light possible. How I treat her, *not* what I think about her behavior, has the most direct impact on everyone watching. When I offer grace and forgiveness, I show the entire class what they can expect if they ever find themselves making a mistake. We were a closer-knit class from this day forward; it was as if the kindness I showed to her was a kindness I showed to all. And she never cut the class again.

We have found that it is often (always?) the case that the students who present the most difficult behaviors to manage are the ones who need us the most. To teach *all* of our students most effectively, we need to be flexible enough to meet students where they are when they need it most. As Costello et al. (2009/2019) note, "being restorative will require you to be creative in your responses to situations that arise in your classroom and your building" (pp. 6–7). In the same way that one strategy for learning may not work for all students, one strategy of discipline may not either. We need to be comfortable in exercising flexibility to meet the needs of students in *each* particular situation.

Cultivating our own flexibility enables us to loosen the reins, give up control, make traditional forms of discipline obsolete, and allow for a classroom in which human dignity is paramount. We want students to feel free to be themselves in the classroom while meeting the expectations we have set for them. Those expectations, whether it is a cell phone policy or a late policy, should be clear to students and explained in a way that demonstrates intentionality and always puts the students first. We want to ensure that students know the space and the time belongs to them. Our profession requires us to serve these students in the ways they need, at any given moment. Thus, our personal commitment to learning how to be fluid and flexible, both in our own minds and in our approach to teaching, is one of the most powerful paths to transformative teaching.

Reflective Activities

- Consider how psychologically flexible you are in your own personal life and in the classroom. In what ways are you still working to increase your flexibility in ways that can benefit your professional practice?

- Are the ways in which you determine yourself to be flexible in the classroom perceived this way by the students? How do you know?

- Complete a mental inventory in which you consider the identity groups of the students whom you have disciplined this year. Are any groups overrepresented? If yes, are there any actions you are taking that may contribute to this? Are there ways in which you can be more flexible in your approach?

- Identify your biggest challenge with student behavior. How does this make you feel and how do you typically react/respond? Do you know why the student engages in this behavior? How could your response better address the motivation for the behavior?

- Consider how you view flexibility in regard to discipline. Why do you view it this way?

References

Costello, B., Wachtel, J., & Wachtel, T. (2009/2019). *The restorative practices handbook for teachers, disciplinarians and administrators*. Bethlehem, PA: International Institute for Restorative Practices.

Danielson, C. (2013). *The framework for teaching evaluation instrument: 2013 edition*. Princeton, NJ: The Danielson Group.

Heavers, K. (2012). *Toward a theory of the educational interruption: A conceptual model of the telling break*. https://doi.org/doi:10.7282/T3B27T7M

Martinez, S. (2009). A system gone berserk: How are zero-tolerance policies really affecting schools? *Preventing School Failure: Alternative Education for Children and Youth, 53*(3), 153–158. https://doi.org/10.3200/PSFL.53.3.153-158

Noddings, N. (2013). *Caring: A relational approach to ethics and moral education*. Berkeley, CA: University of California Press.

11

Maximizing Student Voice and Choice

How to Empower Students Through Greater Autonomy in the Classroom

Our discussions of teacher flexibility and giving up control in the classroom were intentionally placed before this chapter. We hope we have prepared the reader for the topics in this chapter, as they would have been more difficult to implement effectively without our previous emphasis on the importance of releasing control. Similarly, we have argued that the best environment for fostering student vulnerability and risk-taking is a classroom climate in which students feel safe and secure. The structure of this book was designed to build up to this peak, where the reader ideally now feels empowered to exercise the flexibility needed to empower their students.

First, we encourage the reader to reflect upon their teaching methods. Consider the first reflective activity below. In what ways can our students feel more responsible, important, and valued? How can this benefit the learning occurring in our classrooms?

We have already discussed the importance of increasing student voice in the classroom, especially in Chapter 6 as it relates to feedback. We return to it here to emphasize how the valuing and welcoming of student contributions can improve learning for everyone, including the teacher. It can provide new ideas for lessons and promote learning in ways that are both relatable and meaningful for other students, as we know students can better connect to one another than their teachers.

DOI: 10.4324/9781003496588-14

Strategies to Increase Student Voice in the Classroom

As many of us might agree, the most difficult time to speak in front of others is generally the first time. This is true regardless of age and context. With that in mind, it is most beneficial to get students to voice *anything* as early in the year as possible in our classrooms. Introductory activities that allow for low-risk opportunities to engage are a great way to get students to feel comfortable speaking in front of peers. We have asked various low-risk questions (naming one favorite food, sound, color, or animal; choosing one of four images that represent an ideal vacation; identifying a word that resonates with students that day; agreeing or disagreeing with a particular statement) to engage students with us and one another.

Increasing the amount and length of class discussions is another easy way to demonstrate our desire to hear our students. We want to explicitly recognize value in the different experiences of every member of the class. We want to ensure that no voice dominates and also that no "homogenous blob" (as Val's partner would call it) takes over, where differing perspectives are silenced. This open dialogue represents the real world and students need the skill of approaching differences in opinions and values with respect and as much understanding as possible. As Larson and Parker (1996) note, discussion "engages students in *the* essential practice of democratic living" (p. 110).

It is important to ensure that student contributions are *voiced* and can then be *heard* and utilized in a meaningful way in the classroom. We need to establish discussion guidelines and make expectations clear in order for this to occur. Additionally, encouraging students to call on one another in discussions and tasking them with creating the discussion questions can serve the simultaneous goals of increasing student voice *and* choice in the classroom. Providing a routine structure is useful in that it increasingly will allow for less and less teacher involvement in the discussions throughout the school year, as students gain comfort in taking responsibility.

For students who are reluctant or unable to vocalize contributions, we can utilize varied opportunities to contribute such as written or artistic expression. Kate and Val have both had success utilizing technology platforms or discussion features on Google Classroom or Canvas for sharing student ideas. Whiteboards, whether individual or group, can be used to add comments as others are sharing to prevent a student's thoughts from escaping them. Additionally, Kate and Val have privately asked students to read their work aloud if they were unable to or uncomfortable doing so themselves.

Student feedback also serves as a method of honoring student voice. The collection of formal and informal student feedback, especially as it relates to the curriculum, can have a great impact on student engagement. As Conner,

Posner, and Nsowaa (2022) found in their research of 67 urban high schools in Philadelphia, efforts to involve students in negotiating and facilitating the curriculum, what they called "pedagogic voice," resulted in positive student outcomes:

> Not only do students who feel heard more often by their teachers, find school interesting and enjoyable more often, but also they feel cared for and respected by their teachers more often, which in turn leads them [to] work hard more regularly and to find schoolwork meaningful more frequently. Especially in the context of poor school conditions then, student voice—that is, really listening to what students have to say—appears to be a powerful and simple intervention that can yield dividends.
>
> (p. 769)

Kahne, Bowyer, Marshall, and Hodgin (2022) also found various academic benefits, including better grades and attendance, associated with school environments that students regarded as responsive to their critiques. They conclude, "When educators ignore students' voices, one impact may well be democratic and educational disengagement" (p. 410).

Strategies to Increase Student Choice in the Classroom

Again, we want to reiterate the importance of creating the foundation and groundwork for students to feel comfortable when considering allowing students to make learning choices in the first place. For some students, including those who have not been provided options in their learning before, the act of making their own choices in the classroom may initially feel uncomfortable. However, for these students especially, increasing choice in the classroom can be the most beneficial. Starting by allowing for small freedoms, as Kate discusses below, we can help foster student comfortability in independent choice-making in the classroom.

KMH: Today, on the first day of school, a student took out a cookie wrapped in plastic wrap and quietly and carefully ate it right in front of me. I had purposefully decided not to make the first day a bunch of rules and expectations, but I was intentionally giving the overarching ones: self-regulation, safety, and happiness. I wrote these on the board. I asked, "What are we doing about cell phones?" And then I proceeded to explain that I didn't know *where* mine was at the moment. I told them how those of the students who had their phones visible on the desk were using up a part of their cognitive attention on them, the way we are constantly having to give attention to a pet, or a baby, or a nagging friend. I watched them slowly put their phones away. Except for a couple of students. And I didn't mention it. I just noticed it and it was so cool to see who had chosen their own path instead.

I had put the name cards down on the desks in assigned random order so that I could at least see where people sat and confirm their names I'd been studying before school began. One student moved during the first assignment to write answers to the "Introduce yourself" questions. I praised her.

I am intentionally laying the groundwork *early* for students to choose for themselves *all the things within their control* that simply add to their comfort and contentment and that don't disturb anyone in any way. This is what they have already noticed on day one.

We will, for the most part, be able to increase student comfortability with making choices as we continue to let them practice it. Like allowing students to place their phones in areas of their choosing or eat when they are hungry, we can welcome the freedom to make choices that aid in student comfort. When providing options for students, particularly options regarding lesson resources or assessments, we can provide suggestions based on student learning styles and interests. The more we know about our students, the more we can guide them to making choices that will be most meaningful for their learning.

Allowing students to choose resources representing various reading levels, rather than being assigned these, can help students select resources based on their comfort and individual learning needs. Framing different levels of resources as either a "challenge for students who already have background on the topic" or a "more simplified resource for students who are unfamiliar with this topic" may be successful ways to guide students to the most appropriate choices.

Using choice in assessments, as discussed in greater detail later in this chapter, can be another way to incorporate student decision-making into their learning experiences. While traditionally formative and summative assessments do not incorporate many elements of student choice, they can be reworked to do so. Some educators utilize choice boards as one means of supplying structured opportunities for student choice. Taking this concept a step further, educators can encourage students to make their *own* choice boards. Any assessment, really, can be modified once an educator commits to trusting their students to have greater involvement in their own learning. Even if we, as educators, *perceive* students as making an easier or less challenging choice, it is our trusting of the student that matters more than the choice they make. At the same time, the choice they make gives us so much data, including but not limited to: what they have learned from us, what they *haven't* learned from us, how they think of themselves, their preferred learning style, their level of confidence in themselves, and whether they are an accurate judge of their mastery.

Empowerment Through Learning

We recognize that the education system has the potential to increase (true) democracy so long as the teachers/district/system allow it. We need to move beyond the traditional banking model in which knowledge deemed important by the "authority" is deposited into students' brains (Freire, 1970/2018). This model allows students to be passive, stifling creativity and agency. Conversely, what Freire calls problem-posing education permits students to discover reality which can result in the emergence of consciousness and critical intervention. We need such a style of pedagogy if we are to be successful in helping students become their truest and best versions of themselves. As Freire writes, "Problem-posing education affirms men and women as beings in the process of *becoming* – as unfinished, uncompleted beings in and with a likewise unfinished reality" (p. 84). This type of pedagogy that strives to help students understand their agency and motivates them to actively participate in bettering their communities is especially important for students from historically marginalized groups and those living in high-poverty areas (Kahne & Middaugh, 2008).

While the focus on a more problem-based approach can lead to positive outcomes, we would further argue that the individual responsible for helping students build these skills is just as important. Without a teacher that a student can trust and without a classroom in which they feel safe and valued, these lessons will likely fail to be meaningful. A student needs to feel their voice is valued in order to ask the questions and share their experiences which leads to a critical examination of their community and their place in it. Ideally, students should also feel accountable to one another, allowing for a true sense of community.

The goal of empowering students, as described by Ashcroft (1987) as "bringing into a state of belief in one's capability to act effectively," is an important goal in our classrooms. Student empowerment transcends the classroom to other areas of a student's life and will help them to utilize effective citizenship skills moving forward. Glasser (1986) acknowledges that in order to function successfully in a school environment, students must feel that their emotional and intellectual needs are recognized, including their need to assert power. Allowing students to have a sense of control in the classroom provides an important motivator for student productivity, leading to greater personal success for the student as well as a more supportive and engaging classroom environment.

Seeking to empower students is especially important for students who Rubin (2012) classifies as "discouraged" – those who "experience a gap between civic ideals and the realities of their daily lives" (p. 6). She compares these to "empowered" students who have also experienced the gap between civic ideals and reality but remain encouraged to work for change. She has found that certain classroom practices – increased discussions where the teachers "step back," simulations, and targeted writing activities that connect content to student lives – can help push all students, and importantly these "discouraged" students, to experience empowerment.

Using *Authentic Choice Assessments* as Opportunities for Student Agency

While much research has found the benefit of the use of authentic assessments – those with real-world applications that seem more relevant to students' lives – we need to ensure that the students *themselves* find the task to be authentic, as authenticity can be subjective (Gulikers, Bastiaens, & Kirschner, 2004). As Bain (2010) suggests, assessments should "value and validate" student experience and reflect the idea that learning can be constructed more effectively in partnership between student and teacher rather than using traditional teacher-determined methods.

Val, having taught an elective course for many years that was partially populated with students with very low motivation, recognized this "authenticity gap" very clearly. She had heard teachers describe some of her former students as "difficult," "wild," or "sneaky" but, in reality, she found that most of those students just felt disconnected from the content learned in their classes, the routine and rigidity of the school day, and from teachers who seemed (to them at least) to relish in holding control over them. As this became clearer, she experimented with ways to adapt her teaching to meet their needs. She decided to use assessments as a means to help students assume greater ownership of their own learning and, hopefully, increase their motivation.

She began to design assessments around student choice, both in topic and product, and allowed students to choose their own due dates. She called these assessments *authentic choice assessments* and found that each of the choices she made to allow students more control over their learning resulted in higher completion rates, more engagement in the classroom and the community, and more personal growth for the students.

She worked individually with students on project selection days to ensure that the topic choice was substantial enough and, most importantly, meaningful to them. These days were necessary to help them identify and solidify a topic of importance and also to show that she valued setting aside class time to ensure this. As part of a "project introduction worksheet," she asked students to begin researching one topic of interest and accessing resources to explore the topic further. She then asked them to discuss the usefulness of the sources accessed, whether they were still interested in the topic, and whether the topic was too broad or narrow. At this point, she asked the students to finalize their project choice – what they actually wanted to do (write a letter, create a PSA, create art, etc.) – and to determine the next steps to move toward completion. Finally, recognizing that this is potentially non-negotiable in some districts, Val asked her students to select a due date that worked with their plan and schedule as well as hers.

A key piece to this assessment model was student reflection throughout the process. There were four formal opportunities for student reflection, upon their own projects as well as those of their peers. These opportunities allowed them to design and update their completion timelines, experience unique learning opportunities through their peers' projects, and receive structured and unstructured feedback from teachers and peers. During different stages of the project, she used targeted reflection questions to ensure that students were able to engage in metacognition and connection-building. Examples of prompts included the following:

- What did you anticipate would be the most difficult aspect of this project? What actually was the most difficult?
- What was one peer question or comment that helped you to think about your project in a new way?
- Rate your interest and motivation levels for your unit project topic on a 1–10 scale. Explain your ratings.
- What factors contributed to your ability to complete your unit project in the way you intended?
- What, if anything, did you learn about yourself while completing this project?

Workshop days were also incorporated as ways to check in with the teacher and provide continued feedback to move forward. Val was able to observe student progress and guide students to set mini-goals to meet their set deadlines. These days also served as opportunities to network with other students, teachers, and administration.

The assessment then, rather than functioning as merely demonstrating what has already been learned, became a learning process in itself. Students were thinking critically about their own thinking and, on peer sharing days, the learning of their peers. Providing both free and structured reflection activities as a source of learning allowed students to unearth new understandings of their communities and also themselves, rather than just from the teacher-directed content of the course. This process can be liberating for students, as they can ultimately uncover and challenge social issues that impact their own lives. The act of challenging such issues, in whatever way they choose, gives them agency which can be transformative for young people (Freire, 1970/2018).

When Val began teaching American Studies again, she continued to use this *authentic choice assessment* model. Similar to her elective course, she found that students learned about the chosen topic in much greater depth than a traditional assessment may have allowed. Students also overwhelmingly expressed a preference, and often gratitude, for these types of learning experiences. Rather than diverting from the curriculum, it brought more meaning to the content they covered together and she could see student participation and engagement grow in both the classroom and in their communities.

Handing over control of the classroom to students, beyond developing greater motivation, also shows a teacher's trust in the students, which is an important aspect of developing a strong student-teacher relationship. However, this may be difficult for some teachers, particularly those who feel pressure from administration, curriculum, or time constraints, or those who have yet to let go of control over the class. Ultimately though, if we want students to have the best opportunity to be empowered learners, providing student choice and shifting the power dynamic in the classroom is necessary.

Dewey (1916) asserts:

> A primary responsibility of educators is that they not only be aware of the general principle of shaping of actual experience by environing conditions, but that they also recognize in the concrete what surroundings are conducive to having experiences that lead to growth.
>
> (p. 40)

Providing such freedom for students is not without its difficulties, however. It can take a significant amount of time to develop lessons to allow for this, which is why we would propose that administrators provide paid professional development time to allow for the creation of new materials and assessments. Allowing students more freedom with due dates can also pose potential timing issues when it comes to grading deadlines. In the example above, Val was always transparent with students regarding these mandated deadlines and provided suggested due dates for the students, explicitly referencing these deadlines.

Providing opportunities for increased voice and choice empowers students. It essentially unlocks the gates – the barriers that limit students in their learning and thinking – allowing for greater freedom of thought and creative problem-solving. This can, in turn, allow for greater opportunities to improve community, both within and outside of the school, as practicing the opportunity to use one's voice builds confidence to speak on issues outside of the classroom.

Reflective Activities

- Consider how often students are speaking in a typical lesson in your classroom. What is the percentage of lesson time in which you are speaking vs. the students?

- Consider how much choice and responsibility students have in your classroom. What is the percentage of lesson time in which you have control vs. the students having control?

- Choose a unit in your curriculum and consider your unit assessments. Would you have been motivated to complete these assessments as a student? What is the purpose of each? Can the students find meaning in them? What thoughts or questions arise in your consideration of this topic?

- Reflect upon the following discussion questions:
    - To what extent does your classroom serve as a space that promotes democracy?

    - How can you give students a greater voice in your role as an educator?

    - How can you help students to realize their agency?

References

Ashcroft, L. (1987). Defusing "empowering": The what and the why. *Language Arts, 64*(2), 142–156. https://www.jstor.org/stable/41961588

Bain, J. (2010). Integrating student voice: Assessment for empowerment. *Practitioner Research in Higher Education, 4*(1), 14–29. https://files.eric.ed.gov/fulltext/EJ1130598.pdf

Conner, J., Posner, M., & Nsowaa, B. (2022). The relationship between student voice and student engagement in urban high schools. *The Urban Review, 54*(5), 755–774. https://doi.org/10.1007/s11256-022-00637-2

Dewey, J. (1916). *Democracy and education. An introduction to the philosophy of education*. New York: Free Press.

Freire, P. (1970/2018). *Pedagogy of the oppressed*. New York: Bloomsbury.

Glasser, W. (1986). *Control theory in the classroom*. New York: Perennial Library/Harper & Row Publishers.

Gulikers, J. T. M., Bastiaens, T. J., & Kirschner, P. A. (2004). A five-dimensional framework for authentic assessment. *Educational Technology Research and Development, 52*(3), 67–86. http://www.jstor.org/stable/30220391

Kahne, J., Bowyer, B., Marshall, J., & Hodgin, E. (2022). Is responsiveness to student voice related to academic outcomes? Strengthening the rationale for student voice in school reform. *American Journal of Education, 128*(3), 389–415.

Kahne, J., & Middaugh, E. (2008). *Democracy for some: The civic opportunity gap in high school*. Center for Information and Research on Civic Learning and Engagement.

Larson, B. E., & Parker, W. C. (1996). What is classroom discussion? A look at teachers' conceptions. *Journal of Curriculum and Supervision, 11*(2), 110–126.

Rubin, B. C. (2012). *Making citizens: Transforming civic learning for diverse social studies classrooms*. New York: Routledge.

12

Learning Joy

How to Be Intentional About Creating Opportunities of Joy for Ourselves and Our Students

We have saved our discussion of joy for the last chapter. This was an intentional choice, as consistent joy-finding in the classroom – true happiness – would be very difficult to achieve if the teacher remained closed off and the classroom atmosphere felt unsafe. Instead, joy is both a by-product of embracing all of this work and a state of being we can actively seek, knowing that when we do, everyone benefits. What we have discussed in previous chapters – teacher authenticity, demonstrations of vulnerability and caring, a trusting and safe classroom environment, all classroom members committing to a growth mindset and working to reduce stressors – creates a foundation that can allow for joy to flourish in the classroom. We entirely agree with hooks (1994) when she writes, "As a classroom community, our capacity to generate excitement is deeply affected by our interest in one another, in hearing another's voice, in recognizing one another's presence" (p. 8).

Here, again, we ask you to reflect upon your experiences as an educator. Have you considered the role of joy in your professional position? If not, why? How could our practice benefit from moving joy and happiness into our conscious thoughts each day?

The Importance of *Learning Joy*

How would we describe joy? It is larger than happiness, warmer than delight, and feels like a favorite blanket. Johnson (2019) thoughtfully encapsulates the meaning of joy:

Joy involves a state of positive affect, in which one experiences feelings of freedom, safety, and ease. Joy involves changes in visual perception (colors seem brighter), motor behavior (physical movements feel freer and easier, smiling happens involuntarily), and there are characteristic changes in cognition (thinking and attention are broadened and exercised in creative ways).

(p. 6).

Brown (2021) further defines joy as "an intense feeling of deep spiritual connection, pleasure, and appreciation" (p. 205). This connection with the spirit of one human to another reminds us that we are inherently dependent upon our bonds with others in our seeking and experiencing of all kinds of joy. In our classrooms, we are entrusted with growing, nurturing, and teaching human brains, and we know that joy is an essential quality for the brain to experience to build healthy neural connections. Brain-derived neurotrophic factor (BDNF) is integral to the acquisition of new knowledge because it encourages the growth of new cells in the hippocampus of the brain. To simplify this, it is a chemical that links well-being to learning.

Kate has begun using the phrase *learning joy* with her students to name the specific positive emotion one feels upon mastering a skill or acquiring new knowledge that clearly relates to and obviously improves one's life. Keeping an eye out for a brain discovering a new thing is a way to find it. Find the face and hear the exclamation of a young person who has just recognized a new pattern or found an answer to a problem that had them stumped, and you will witness palpable *learning joy*. Once a person has felt this feeling and has named it, their whole experience of being in a classroom can shift. Suddenly, the learner finds themselves in control of a process that will build upon itself and bring greater and greater sources of joy. This process feeds upon itself in the healthiest way. Just as a video game motivates a person through the visual and auditory rewards it supplies, a student in a classroom is enabled to find this feeling as they learn new skills and knowledge, and they will be motivated to continue this pursuit.

This brings us to the importance of naming joy. Johnson (in Brown, 2021) explains, "cultures that have more words to describe the emotion of joy may also experience joy more richly" (p. 205). As we have discussed in earlier chapters, naming emotions is one of the fundamental skills required for self-reflection and growth. Brackett (2019) argues, "one of the five skills for becoming an 'emotional scientist' is to learn to label emotions with a nuanced vocabulary" (p. 19). Even though this is a relatively new idea, we are learning that to be able to put a name to these subtly different positive emotions that occur in the classroom will mean experiencing them more frequently. Asking students to write about their experiences using these words further helps to solidify these feelings and experiences. Identifying one's intentionality here can not only enhance the experience of joy, but it can demonstrate to students that we care about their happiness and emotional well-being.

Moments of joy may be easier to identify in elementary school as younger children are more likely than older children to embrace silliness and less likely to mask their enthusiasm for fear of ridicule. Our goal then becomes to maximize the joy so that as many students as possible can experience it and to teach in ways that bring back the comfort of displaying the experience of joy for students of all ages. These experiences are not just useful in relationship-building and community-building, but they provide opportunities to learn new cognitive and behavioral skills and enhance resilience (Hartmann, Weiss, Hoegl, & Carmeli, 2021; Johnson, 2019).

Humor, when used appropriately, can also be a way to inspire such joy. As Savage, Lujan, Thipparthi, and DiCarlo (2017) remind us, "humor creates an environment that promotes learning" by reducing anxiety, enhancing participation, and increasing motivation, and humor related to course material can attract and sustain student attention (p. 341). We might refer to this as *laughing joy*, a subtly different but no less valuable classroom emotion.

Since we are all unique individuals, what feels like joy will vary too. That being said, despite the fact that it might be obvious, thinking about how we nurture ourselves in our own joy, so we can cultivate it in our classrooms, is a worthwhile endeavor. It can impact the engagement, motivation, sense of belongingness, emotional and physical health, and ultimately, the very futures of our students and ourselves. When we really consider the profound impacts of this feeling, it becomes difficult to deny that it is a necessity in the classroom.

Encouraging Joy in Educators

The way in which a teacher conveys the importance of content can help students to feel the joy of learning or conversely dampen the joy a young person feels in the classroom. If you have lost the joy or interest in your subject, seek it out. Val has attended week-long seminars through Gilder Lehrman and the Korea Academy for Educators. Each reinspired her teaching and she cherished the discussions and experiences with teachers from around the country. Kate was able to meet and work with scientists and authors at Princeton University's QUEST Program, deepening her knowledge of geology, the origin of life, and molecular clocks in evolution in addition to learning from astrophysicists. Through this program, she also explored climate change and ways to incorporate the most recent research into the biology curriculum. We would hope that anyone in school leadership would encourage these opportunities by providing teachers with funding and information. These learning opportunities are investments that ultimately benefit the students, as a teacher who can convey enthusiasm and excitement has a greater capacity to inspire.

We also recognize the importance of teacher preferences in choosing and designing their courses. Each of us has favorite courses/levels to teach and leaning into those benefits everyone, but most especially the students. Kate feels honored to have taught human anatomy and physiology and biology for nearly 25 years at the high school level. While she was assigned these courses early in her career, these became her preferred courses to teach. Val, who prefers to teach the history of the United States (ideally the most recent years), even made this known when interviewing. We recognize that we are more effective as educators when we adore our content areas. Again, anyone in a school leadership position should note that acknowledging and acting upon such teacher preferences benefits the learning experience for all.

Incorporating Joy into Curricula

In 2021, during a conference Val attended run by the organization Facing History, Dr. Gholdy Muhammad built upon her educational framework (the HILL model), suggesting that joy should explicitly be incorporated into our lessons and curricula. She expands upon this concept in her latest (beautifully designed) book, *Unearthing Joy*, where she provides practical tools and resource examples to incorporate the pursuit of joy into lesson and unit plans (Muhammad, 2023). This intentional call to see the joy in ourselves and others can be especially affirming for students of historically marginalized groups who may only see themselves represented in curricula in limited ways if at all.

Over the years, Val's discussions with students and community groups have confirmed the importance of explicit discussions of the joys and successes of various groups of people who have been historically marginalized. Students have expressed a loss of connection with the content as well as the teacher as a result of not having their identities represented positively in the classroom. Reworking our lessons to intentionally represent the experiences and the joys of all communities can help remedy this situation.

As examples, we can incorporate art, music, literature, nature, dance, and/or discussion of celebrations into our lessons. We can connect positive aspects of our students' lives to the content we teach. Muhammad (2023) suggests that our lessons should include objectives related to joy and a family/home connection in addition to ones related to identity, skill, intellect, and criticality. For example, when teaching the state standard in which students identify the Star-Spangled Banner as the national anthem of the United States, she suggests expanding beyond the requisite learning of this anthem by including the following objectives for identity, joy, and family/home connection:

> **Identity:** Students will identify songs that give them self-pride.
> **Joy:** Students will learn about the song, "Lift Every Voice and Sing," and the beauty in it.
> **Family/Home Connection:** As a family, make a playlist of songs that lift our joy.
>
> (p. 49)

The communication of joy or the absence of joy in the curriculum can work in powerful ways in regard to student motivation and relationship-building and therefore would be meaningful for teachers to reflect upon. We encourage you to examine this with some of the reflective questions below.

Recently Val asked her student teachers to discuss the moments of joy they experienced during the semester. Nearly all of the experiences discussed were spontaneous occurrences in the classroom, unplanned yet welcomed by these pre-service teachers. It is worth noting that teacher flexibility is also important as it relates to moments in the classroom that can bring or shut down opportunities for shared joy.

Many opportunities for joy can be intercepted by teachers rushing to get through the curriculum or fearing an administrator walking by and seeing a class off task. But these are the moments we remember and these are the moments we need. The time when a student accidentally calls us "mom" and then everyone begins sharing when they accidentally called other people "mom." The time a student walks into class with their headphones too loud and starts an accidental dance party. The time we include a travel photo in our content presentation and students start sharing their favorite travel stories. The time when we make a "dad joke" but then students don't find it funny and then *that* becomes funny so everyone starts laughing. (Val's dad has the best dad jokes. She has used them in class often.)

Whether spontaneous or woven into the lesson, joy should be a common occurrence in the classroom. We have been privileged to have had teaching careers where we felt this often and we wish that for our readers and their future students as well.

We need to lean into the joy, welcome the joy, cultivate the joy.

Reflective Activities

- Think about the last lesson you taught. Were there any moments of joy? How can you create more opportunities for this?

- Respond to the following questions asked by Muhammad (2023, p. 77):
  - "How is joy amplified in each of my unit plans?"

  - "Why do students need this type of joy?"

- Discuss with a colleague:
  - What brings you joy? Who knows this about you? Should more people know this?

  - What are some of your memorable moments of *learning joy*?

References

Brackett, M. (2019). *Permission to feel: The power of emotional intelligence to achieve well-being and success.* New York: Celadon Books.

Brown, B. (2021). *Atlas of the heart: Mapping meaningful connection and the language of human experience* (1st ed.). New York: Random House.

Hartmann, S., Weiss, M., Hoegl, M., & Carmeli, A. (2021). How does an emotional culture of joy cultivate team resilience? A sociocognitive perspective. *Journal of Organizational Behavior, 42,* 313–331. https://doi.org/10.1002/job.2496

hooks, b. (1994). *Teaching to transgress: Education as the practice of freedom.* London: Routledge.

Johnson, M. K. (2019). Joy: A review of the literature and suggestions for future directions. *The Journal of Positive Psychology, 15*(1), 5–24. https://doi.org/10.1080/17439760.2019.1685581

Muhammad, G. (2023). *Unearthing joy: A guide to culturally and historically responsive teaching and learning.* New York: Scholastic.

Savage, B. M., Lujan, H. L., Thipparthi, R. R., & DiCarlo, S. E. (2017). Humor, laughter, learning, and health! A brief review. *Advances in Physiology Education, 41*(3), 341–347. https://doi.org/10.1152/advan.00030.2017

Conclusion
Sojourners Together

This book, particularly the latter portion, highlights the importance of individual reflective work in order to be able to participate meaningfully in a community. As hooks (2003) notes, "Finding out what connects us, revelling in our differences; this is the process that brings us closer, that gives us a world of shared values, of meaningful community" (p. 197). We must know ourselves in order to participate in this process – to find our connections and differences. Demonstrating our true authentic selves will help us to gain the trust and respect of others to work together in ways that allow for the opportunities that can only come with vulnerability and risk-taking.

While we know that working alone may result in a product delivered more quickly, it seldom produces the *best* product. Garrison (1996) acknowledges the importance of shared dialogue in developing a person for the better when he states "changes in identity are not a matter of 'willing' oneself to change. It takes critical self-reflection and the kind of intelligence that can only come from shared inquiry" (p. 439). These personal changes in the teacher and the students can only be achieved *together*. We need others to provide insight and feedback, to question and push thinking. Writing this book with two authors serves as a perfect example. While we know we are capable of writing alone, the synergistic nature of our shared writing experience reinforces for us the richness that comes from shared thinking. We each put forth our unique ideas and the experience is enriched by listening to one another critically and having to create united thought.

VK: "*E pluribus unum*: out of many, one." Each year of my high school teaching career I participated in our school's Washington Seminar program. Each year I sat with my dear colleague-turned-friend and listened to the narrator of the introductory video for the Capitol building tour say these words. One year I commented on how much I loved the narrator's voice when she spoke these words, and afterward "*E pluribus unum*: out of many, one" became a phrase we would repeat to each other throughout the trip and ultimately throughout the year. The phrase, a beautiful representation of the connectedness of a country's people, also can represent the profession of education. We – as educators, as individuals, as classes, as a school – succeed more easily when we work together, when we belong to a community.

In 2011, while on a teacher grant to study the Atlantic slave trade in Barbados, I saw a paper sign stapled to the bulletin board in one of UWI's dormitory buildings. The message read, "No you, no me, but we." I took a photo of the sign because it resonated with me. The process of learning, and of teaching, is about building together.

Now that I have "retired" from full-time teaching, I miss the feeling of being "in it together" with my colleagues – that feeling that can only come with a high-stress job. Yet, even thousands of miles and years removed, I still feel "one" with them, like I could jump back in and pick up where I left off. I attribute that feeling to the vulnerability I allowed myself to have as a teacher that helped to foster these deep, meaningful connections.

KMH: In a recent conversation with my mother, I asked her, "What are things I need to know?"

She answered, "Treat your students how you wish for them to *be*. Model for your students how to be, and they will be that way."

I had not been sure that Mama, who lives with dementia, still remembered that I was a teacher. I had given her no clues, no reminders. I was just curious about what she would say and had zero expectations that it would be anything so profound. But there it was. My mother, ever the teacher, ever the loving parent and guide, offered the most universal wisdom of all, that we teach from who we are. I see clearly now that we are each a link in a long chain, held together one to the next, by love.

Freire (1970/2018) discusses how the move to problem-posing education replaces the dynamic of teacher-of-the-students and students-of-the-teacher with teacher-student and students-teachers. This joint responsibility for the success in the classroom is what we aim for. Rather than the teacher being removed from learning, we are all learning together. We are sojourners together. We are seeking truth together. We are seeking growth and improvement and wholeness together. We are achieving these goals and dreams *together*.

Anyone who taught during the pandemic knows the necessity of teaching in community. The turmoil of those years brought a whole new meaning of togetherness. Many of us and our students experienced loss – both individually and communally – and we navigated the path *together*.

We have discussed in Chapter 8 how our journeys ideally become intertwined with those of our colleagues, providing mutual, and much-needed, support. Relationships rooted in respect, support, and collaboration not only function as support for faculty but also as networks to support students and model for them healthy working relationships. These relationships can help us to look inward and also to see ourselves from the outside, maybe in ways we had not previously seen.

Beyond our individual efforts to connect with students and colleagues, we agree with researchers like Perry (2006/2017) who argue that school systems need to change in order to address students' emotional and physical needs, rather than focusing solely on cognitive development. We need to explicitly build in time for social interaction and free play and emphasize the practice of relational skills. We need to move toward restorative practices as opposed to traditional discipline. We need to consider scheduling and the potential of looping to best benefit student-teacher relationships (Wedenoja, Papay, & Kraft, 2022).

We are all growing. The writing of this book has changed us, just as reading it has changed you. We recognize that being a human is the work of being in flux. Our brains are *always* changing. The more we embrace change and growth, with the support of those around us, the more comfortable we can become in the uncomfortable journeys ahead.

So many people have participated in our journeys and we are grateful for each of them. We may have shared space temporarily or have chosen to extend our bonds for life. Either way, we have grown because of these relationships, and we hope this growth has been mutual. The gift of these relationships was only possible because of our intentional choice to open up our minds and hearts and allow others in. As we remove the barriers to human connection, we can more easily see the universality of our shared light. In turn, this illumination of who we *all* are enables us to transform our practice.

References

Freire, P. (1970/2018). *Pedagogy of the oppressed*. New York: Bloomsbury.

Garrison, J. (1996). A Deweyan theory of democratic listening. *Educational Theory, 46*, 429–451. https://doi.org/10.1111/j.1741-5446.1996.00429.x

hooks, b. (2003). *Teaching community: A pedagogy of hope*. New York: Routledge.

Perry, B. (2006/2017). *The boy who was raised as a dog and other stories from a child psychiatrist's notebook: What traumatized children can teach us about loss, love, and healing*. New York: Basic Books.

Wedenoja, L., Papay, J. P., & Kraft, M. A. (2022). *Second time's the charm? How sustained relationships from repeat student-teacher matches build academic and behavioral skills*. https://edworkingpapers.com/sites/default/files/ai22-590.pdf

For Product Safety Concerns and Information please contact our EU representative GPSR@taylorandfrancis.com
Taylor & Francis Verlag GmbH, Kaufingerstraße 24, 80331 München, Germany

www.ingramcontent.com/pod-product-compliance
Lightning Source LLC
Chambersburg PA
CBHW081148230426
43664CB00018B/2841